GHOSTHUNTING
OHIO

AMERICA'S
HAUNTED ROAD TRIP

Titles in the *America's Haunted Road Trip* Series:

Ghosthunting Colorado
Ghosthunting Florida
Ghosthunting Kentucky
Ghosthunting Illinois
Ghosthunting Maryland
Ghosthunting Michigan
Ghosthunting New Jersey
Ghosthunting New York City
Ghosthunting North Carolina
Ghosthunting Ohio
Ghosthunting Ohio: On the Road Again
Ghosthunting Oregon
Ghosthunting Pennsylvania
Ghosthunting San Antonio, Austin, and Texas Hill Country
Ghosthunting Southern California
Ghosthunting Southern New England
Ghosthunting Texas
Ghosthunting Virginia

Chicago Haunted Handbook
Cincinnati Haunted Handbook
Nashville Haunted Handbook
Haunted Hoosier Trails
More Haunted Hoosier Trails
Spirits of New Orleans
Spooked in Seattle
Twin Cities Haunted Handbook

GHOSTHUNTING
OHIO

John B. Kachuba

CLERISY PRESS

Ghosthunting Ohio

For further information, contact the publisher at:
  Clerisy Press
  An imprint of AdventureKEEN
  306 Greenup Street
  Covington, KY 41011
  www.clerisypress.com

Library of Congress Cataloging-in-Publication Data
Kachuba, John B., 1950–
  Ghosthunting Ohio / John B. Kachuba.
    p. cm. — (The haunted heartland series)
  isbn 10: 1-57860-181-9 (pbk.); isbn 13: 978-1-57860-181-3 (pbk.)
  isbn 978-1-57860-401-2 (ebook); isbn 978-1-57860-594-1 (hardcover)
  1. Haunted places—Ohio. 2. Ghosts—Ohio. I. Title. II. Series.

bf1472.u6k33   2004
133.1'09771—dc22   2004053238

Manufactured in the United States of America
Distributed by Publishers Group West

Editor: Jessica Yerega
Cover and interior design: Kelly N. Kofron

Cover and interior photos provided John B. Kachuba, with the following exceptions: p. 73 courtesy of Rider's Inn; p. 81 courtesy of Warehouse on the Canal; p. 150 courtesy of Heritage Village Museum in Cincinnati, Ohio; p. 154 courtesy of The Golden Lamb; pps. 163, 165, and 169 courtesy of Hilton Cincinnati, Netherland Plaza; p. 172 courtesy of Taffy's Main Street Café; p. 184 courtesy of The Vernon Manor Hotel

CONTENTS

ABOUT THE AUTHOR

John B. Kachuba is the author (with his wife, Mary A. Newman, Ph.D.) of *Why is this Job Killing Me?* and *How to Write Funny*. His short fiction and nonfiction have been widely published. He is a recent winner of the Dogwood Fiction Prize and has been published in such journals as *Tin House, Hawaii Pacific Review, Connecticut Review, Mississippi Quarterly*, and others. He holds advanced degrees in creative writing from Antioch University and Ohio University. He currently lives in Athens, Ohio.

Introduction

There are more things in heaven and earth,
Horatio, than are dreamt of in your philosophy.
—*Hamlet,* William Shakespeare

YOU MAY HAVE NEVER SEEN A GHOST. You may not even believe in the existence of spirits. Yet, I would wager that you have, at one time or another, felt a shiver course down your spine when alone in the dark. You have quickly walked through a cemetery at night, not daring to look behind you. Certainly, you have turned on several lights when left in the house by yourself. And you would never go down into the basement alone.

Never.

Why? What is it that makes you afraid?

That was the question I was trying to answer as I wrote this book. What is this irrational fear of the dark, of being alone, of old houses and cemeteries, all about? Is it caused by supernatural entities? Do ghosts walk among us, chilling us to the bone?

You may be skeptical about the existence of ghosts, but it is difficult to disregard the fact that almost every culture around the world has a body of ghost stories and that the particulars of these stories are so similar. Such stories have been around for centuries, and new ones are constantly being added. Perhaps we can make allowances for the ancient stories by chalking them up to a lack of education and sophistication in primitive societies, but how do we, in our modern, technologically advanced society, explain the new stories? Technology, in fact, has added a whole new dimension to paranormal research. Investigators use photography, sound recordings, and electromagnetic sensors to validate their claims for the existence of spirits.

There are experiences that defy logic, science, and technology, strange occurrences for which we have no explanation. I cannot explain the whitish orbs that appeared in some photos I took in buildings said to be haunted. I cannot explain the feelings of negative energy I felt in a haunted basement.

Perhaps ghosts do exist.

One way to find out, I thought, was to visit places where ghosts have been reported. Since I live in Athens, Ohio, described over the years by several experts in paranormal research as one of the most haunted locations in the world, I had a good base from which to start my explorations. Eventually, they would take me on journeys throughout the state of Ohio. I explored historic homes, convents, libraries, inns, prisons, forts, cemeteries, museums, and other assorted odd locations, all said to be haunted.

Often my wife, Mary, would accompany me on these ramblings, so we were able to trade notes and compare our experiences. I went to each of these places with an open mind and no preconceived notions about the existence of ghosts. I have read too many books about hauntings from writers who see ghosts on every street corner and, frankly, find them unbelievable. I am not a "sensitive," or medium. I'm an average guy, just like you, with a curiosity about things paranormal. My intentions as I wrote this book were to accurately and objectively describe for you my observations and experiences, as well as the experiences of others I met along the way, and then let you draw your own conclusions.

Each of the locations described in this book are open to the public, so I encourage you to visit them and explore them for yourself. Some may require calling ahead for appointments; others may only be open on certain days during the week. Check the Travel Guide section in the back of this book for complete information. The guide also gives you maps and directions to each location, as well as important travel tips about them.

Here are some guidelines that may be helpful to you as you begin ghosthunting:

1. **Conduct all your investigations with an open mind, but don't let yourself be fooled by the "evidence."** No one has yet been able to scientifically prove or disprove the existence of ghosts, and it's unlikely you will be the one to earn that fame. Better to simply be nonjudgmental and open to whatever you experience and observe for yourself. Be hard-nosed about the "evidence" you uncover. Make certain that you exhaust all possible explanations before you claim a brush with the supernatural.

2. **Interview other witnesses separately**. Take a page from standard police procedurals and always talk to witnesses of paranormal phenomena separately so that one witness's testimony does not influence that of another.

3. **Document your activities.** I always carry a notebook and pen, tape recorder, and camera with me when investigating a site. The tape recorder is used to interview witnesses, but some people have also used it to record background sound over a period of time to try and catch unidentifiable sounds or voices in a particular location.

   A note about photography is important here. Many people, using either traditional or digital cameras, have reported various anomalies on the photos once they are developed or downloaded into a computer. These anomalies—usually whitish orbs, but also misty smears—are invisible to the naked eye when the photo is taken. There are many reasonable explanations for these objects. They may be dust particles or water droplets on the camera lens. They may be reflections caused by the flash of other cameras or by common objects—even some insects—that the photographer simply did not notice at the time. Your finger, or the camera strap covering part of the camera lens, may also be possible explanations for your photogenic ghost. Enlarging the photo will often help you identify the anomaly accurately. Despite all these reasonable explanations, there are hundreds of "ghost photos" that defy explanation—much to my surprise, I have taken some myself while writing this book.

4. **Respect the site.** It is important to remember that any haunted site carries with it a history of both the people who inhabited the site and of the site itself. That history is worthy of your respect. You should observe whatever rules and regulations might be in effect for the site and work within them. In other words, you should not be breaking into buildings or removing anything from them as souvenirs. Nor should you be prowling around cemeteries after posted hours. You will find that people are more receptive to helping you with your explorations if you follow the rules.

5. **Respect the privacy of your contacts.** Some people may tell you their own ghost stories, but for a variety of reasons, may not want other people to know their identity. You must respect their right to privacy. Unless noted otherwise, all the names of the persons appearing in this book are real. I told all my contacts that I was writing a book and asked for permission to use their real names. If permission was not granted—which was rare—or if I was unable to obtain a name for some reason, I told their stories using pseudonyms. These pseudonyms are identified in the text by an (*) after the name.

6. **Be a knowledgeable ghosthunter.** This last point is perhaps the most important one. No one really knows the rules and laws of the spirit world. Ghosthunters are always exploring *terra incognita* and finding their way by learning from others, but it is important to learn from

those who are serious about their work, rather than from people who are merely looking for kicks. Serious ghosthunters, such as Ed and Lorraine Warren, who wrote this book's epilogue, emphasize that knowledge about ghosts and the spirit world will increase your chances of obtaining your goals but, more important, will keep you safe. The Warrens and other top psychic investigators never resort to dubious psychic "tools," such as the Ouija board, which can, in inexperienced hands, summon unwanted and uncontrollable spirits. I urge you to read and learn from the experts before venturing forth on your own ghosthunting expedition.

I have met many interesting people along the way as I wrote this book. To all of you—too many to list individually—who shared your stories with me, or helped me with accommodations and resources, I extend my most sincere gratitude. This book could not have been written without you.

For all my readers, I hope that *Ghosthunting Ohio* will be a useful guide for you as you explore the world of the paranormal. Please feel free to contact me through my publisher if you would like to share your experiences with me.

Happy hunting!

John B. Kachuba
Athens, Ohio

Northwest

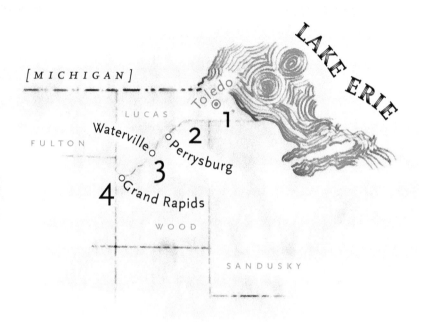

[MICHIGAN]

LAKE ERIE

LUCAS

FULTON

Waterville

Toledo

Perrysburg

1

2

3

Grand Rapids

4

WOOD

SANDUSKY

Collingwood Arts Center

TOLEDO

IN HIS ROLE AS EXECUTIVE DIRECTOR of the Collingwood Arts Center, Tom Brooks is used to working long hours and to having unexpected visitors drop by. People are curious about the arts center and the fortunate painters, potters, and musicians who reside in the huge Romanesque brick mansion. It was first used by the Roman Catholic Ursuline sisters as a school in 1905, served later as Mary Manse College, and was finally used as the nuns' convalescent and retirement center.

Tom remembers a day in August 2003 when three elderly visitors, a man and two women, showed up at his office just as he was about to leave for the day.

"The women were retired nuns who had lived here back in the early fifties," Tom said. "They were reminiscing about the building, remembering the layout from those days and how much it had changed. We were chatting about the art center's former life when one of the nuns suddenly asked me if the shadow was still in the basement."

The nun was referring to a dark, shadowy figure that some people have seen stalking the basement tunnels and the staircases leading up to the first floor. Current residents of the arts center call the thing Shadow Man, although the nun believed the being was a woman, the ghost of Sister Angelique, who had hung herself in the basement many years ago.

"She said that the nuns would never go down into the basement alone," Tom said. "It was creepy listening to her. She was talking about 1952, 1953—and here it is 2003, and people are still seeing the thing."

Tom has seen flashes of light from the corner of his eye, a phenomenon shared by other residents of Collingwood, although he has never seen Shadow Man.

But Mike Hooper has seen it. Several times.

"The most recent time was when I was standing on the steps to the basement with my friend and we felt a person walk past us," Mike said. "It came right up the stairs and felt like a cold breeze going through us. I got tingly all through my body. There was no one there. It was a perfect silhouette of a person, a dark silhouette, but you could definitely see movement within it."

Mike, who is a resident photographer at Collingwood, has also taken photographs inside the building that reveal orbs of light when developed or downloaded into a computer. Tom, who is also a photographer, has captured the orbs on film as well. Many people believe that such orbs, invisible to the naked eye when the picture is taken, are some form of energy that indicates the presence of spirits.

The day my wife, Mary, and I visited the Collingwood Arts Center did not seem conducive to seeing spirits. Bright sunshine, not a single cloud in the deep blue sky. Rising several stories above the trees on Collingwood Boulevard, the gray brick mansion is an imposing landmark in Toledo's old east side and was easy to find. We were early for our appointment with Tom so we had time to take in the details of the beautiful old building: elaborate brickwork in herringbone and dovetail designs, a large Romanesque arch over the entryway, row upon row of windows ascending toward the tile roof (which was under repair at the time, covered with tarps and surrounded by scaffolding). The long rectangular building is set sideways on the lot so that one of the short ends faces the street.

Between the arts center and the street is an intricately designed high Victorian house, known as the Gerber House. Built by wealthy merchant Christian Gerber in 1872, the house is now physically connected to the arts center and is used as artists' residences and for public receptions. Another Victorian house, gutted and in disrepair, stands nearby. Called the Tea House, it also is owned by the arts center.

We tried the door to the arts center but it was locked. One of the men working on the roof was exiting the building and let us in. It was cool and quiet inside, a relief from the bright sunshine and heat outside. There was no one around. We were in a vestibule, a long hallway opening through double doors on either side. We walked through one of the halls, noting its row of arched windows that overlooked a small courtyard. On the other side of the hall, tall wooden doors with transom windows of snowflake-patterned glass opened into artists' studios, formerly classrooms.

We walked back the way we had come, crossed the vestibule, and entered the opposite hall. Old classrooms, now used as offices by various community groups, lined the hall. Artwork hung on the walls, a variety of styles and subjects, painted by resident artists. I snapped a picture in the hall.

With its towering doors and dark woodwork, the hall reminded me of a parochial school I had attended as a youth. I could almost see the dour nuns in their black habits keeping a stern watch over their students as they entered the classrooms. Tom's office was located in that hall but it was locked, so Mary and I waited without speaking, as if we were afraid to disturb the stillness around us.

After a few minutes Tom showed up and unlocked his office. Before we toured the building, he said, he had something he wanted to show us. He turned on the computer and brought up some photos he had taken inside Collingwood. There were the orbs. They had been taken in various locations throughout the building—in his office, the halls, the theater, and, of course, the basement. Solid white spheres, like cue balls, bluish-green ones, an orange one sitting in an easy chair.

"I'm something of a skeptic when it comes to spirits," Tom said, "but I can't explain these orbs. I've been a photographer for some time, and I can't find any reasonable explanation for them. Dust, water, reflections, nothing makes sense."

Tom turned off the computer. Mike Hooper joined us just as we were about to start off on our tour. As we walked up to the second floor I asked Mike what had sparked his interest in exploring the paranormal at Collingwood.

"Things began happening to me almost as soon as I moved in several months ago," he said.

"Like what?"

"Like waking up in the middle of the night to see my deodorant spinning around crazily on my dresser. Hearing a voice say, 'Good night,' when there was no one there. Doors slamming in my face, that kind of thing."

Any one of which, had I experienced it, would have had me packing my bags.

But even stranger things have happened to Mike. One night he and some friends at Collingwood were playing around with a Ouija board—a practice, by the way, considered dangerous by many paranormal investigators because of the bad spirits that can come through.

"We asked it, 'Why are you here?'" Mike said, "and the answer came back immediately, not on the board, but in a clear voice right over our heads. 'To help you find the answer,' it said."

We walked up the stairs.

"These are the doors I was talking about," Mike said as our group arrived at the second floor.

A pair of French doors stood open at the entrance to the hall.

"One time as I was walking towards them they started to swing closed and suddenly slammed shut," Mike said. "I grabbed the knob, but I couldn't turn it. I twisted it hard. It wouldn't budge. It was like something was holding it from the other side. I stepped back, and then tried it again. The door opened easily. It really freaked me out."

We walked through the doorway and down the hall. I kept waiting to hear the doors bang closed behind us.

We entered a dimly lit narrow passage that connected to the Gerber House. In the passage was a beautifully turned walnut staircase leading to the upper floors. I looked up through the stairwell and was startled to see a human leg protruding into the air two floors up. It took me a moment to realize that the leg was not human at all, but part of a mannequin. I could see that the walls on some of the upper floors were in deteriorating condition, some of them revealed down to the lathing.

Sunlight flooded the front rooms of the Gerber House, streaming in through the tall windows, shining on the Eastlake fireplace and mirror surround, intricately carved in burl walnut. A children's art show had recently been presented in the airy parlor of the house and the artwork was still taped helter-skelter to the walls. Superheroes. Animals. Families. The usual subject matter of juvenile artists. The exhibit may have been quite fitting for the Gerber House, since some say the spirits of children can be seen running in and out of the closets there. Although the resident artists can only speculate about the origin of the young spirits, no doubt they would appreciate such pictures.

We retraced our steps from the Gerber House and came back into the main building. The hall curved and we found ourselves standing behind the balcony section of the theater. Thin shafts of light slanted through the archway to our left, leading to an exit. On our right, the gloomy darkness of the theater lay below us. Despite the stained-glass dome that rises above the theater, it was dark. In the dim light, I could pick out the two baroque canopies over miniature stages that were once box seats.

"The spirit of a nun is said to be in here," Tom said.

"Third row, balcony, stage left," Mike said. "That's where she always sits. Performers will sometimes say they see her watching when no one else is in the theater."

I had been taking pictures throughout our tour and took one looking down into the theater, even though I didn't think there was enough light to make a good photo.

From the theater we headed back to Tom's office, coming unexpectedly upon the disturbing life-sized statue of Saint Angela Merici, founder of the Ursuline order, oddly placed on the stairway landing between the second and first floors. The glass block window set in the landing behind the statue provided only pale light.

"Visitors are always startled when they come upon her," Mike said.

The face of the statue had a weird waxy look to it that seemed somehow alive. The eyes looked right through me.

"I've seen her turn her head," Mike said.

Looking into her eyes, it seemed entirely possible.

Mike had other business and left us when we reached Tom's office.

"What about the basement?" I asked. "Can we see that?"

Tom seemed surprised by our request, but he complied. Snatching up some keys from his desk, he led the way into the vestibule where Mary and I had first entered the building. He unlocked an unmarked door below the staircase and flicked on a light switch.

We stood looking down into the basement, upon the stairs where Mike had seen the Shadow Man. A walnut handrail was bolted to the wall on the right side of the stairs. Below the left-side handrail was an ornate open filigree design of metal work that resembled the staircase of some elegant old hotel ballroom. Tom said the rail was valued at several thousand dollars, but it was out of place with the torn up, littered floor at the bottom and the naked light bulb hanging at the foot of the stairs. The bulb created a cone of yellow light, but all was darkness around it. I paused and took a picture looking down the stairs as Mary and Tom descended into the basement.

The basement was entirely what one would expect of a large institution that had seen better times. Dark and dirty. Musty. Workrooms and storage rooms filled with dusty machinery and tools, artists' supplies, old stage sets, cobwebbed old cupboards containing who knew what. One room held nothing but glass globes that were the building's original light fixtures. Another contained the original telephone system, a complicated network of wires, switches, and relays that took up an entire wall; the new system occupied an area only a few square feet. Tom turned on lights as we went through the labyrinth of basement tunnels. Here was the laundry, the kitchen, the bakery with its huge baking ovens, more storage rooms, one room sealed off behind a wall that no one has yet been able to enter.

We came to a large open space the resident artists use as a

lounge. A beat-up old sofa and a round table with half a dozen mismatched chairs were the only furnishings in the inhospitable place. Someone had painted several red skull-like images on the support posts and the floor. No one knows who painted them or why, but some speculate that it could have been the work of an occult group who may have used the building during the several years it stood derelict, between the closing of the nuns' retirement home and the opening of the arts center. No artist relaxed in the poorly lit lounge when we were there. I couldn't imagine anyone ever relaxing there.

We headed back to the stairs we had descended. Just before we got there we passed through a dark section of tunnel. Mary and Tom were only a few feet ahead of me in the darkness, although I could not see them. Suddenly, I felt an overwhelming sense of anxiety, tension I had not felt before. It seemed that my heart was racing, my skin felt prickly, as if someone were nearby. I had the urge to look behind me but did not. I forced myself to keep walking. As suddenly as those feelings came over me, they disappeared. It was as though I had walked through a cloud of negative energy. Neither Tom nor Mary felt anything in the basement.

We left Collingwood and, later that night, I downloaded my photos into the computer. I was stunned. Orbs appeared in several photos. One large greenish-blue orb at the precise location in the theater said to be haunted by the nun, one in the front

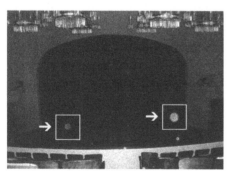

Orbs in the theater at Collingwood Arts Center.

parlor window of the Gerber House, and one at the foot of the basement stairs, just where I had experienced those strange sensations. Just like Tom and Mike, I am at a loss to explain their presence.

The Collingwood Arts Center is an active and vibrant arts community, bringing both visual and performing arts to the public, and encouraging and supporting local talents in their growth as artists. There is a strong energy there, the energy of many creative people working together. Could it be that some of that energy may be generated by the spirits of Collingwood as they try to help the artists "find the answer" to their own artistic questions?

Columbian House

WATERVILLE

TIME PASSES SLOWLY IN THE LITTLE TOWN OF WATER-
VILLE. At Columbian House it seems to have stopped completely.
The three-story clapboard building sits at the corner of River Road
and Farnsworth Road, the words "Columbian House" emblazoned
across the triple door façade in letters two-feet high. John Pray,
Waterville's founder, built the structure in 1828, originally to serve
as a trading post. It has been a prominent local landmark since
then and is now listed on the National Register of Historic Places.

The inn's many windows gaze sleepily out onto the street.
They have seen a fantastic parade of humanity over the last 175
years that reflects the transformation of the rough and tumble

old Northwest Territory into modern-day Ohio. Pioneers and traders, Indians and soldiers, peddlers and drunks, gamblers and politicians. The inn has seen them all.

"Even if you forget all about the ghost stories associated with Columbian House, the place is interesting and important from an historical point of view," Tom Parker told me when I spoke with him on the telephone to arrange a visit with him. Parker, along with his wife, Peggy, and daughter, Meredith, owns and operates the inn.

But you can't forget about the ghosts.

A framed 1995 article from the *Toledo Blade,* detailing the ghostly history of Columbian House, is proudly displayed on an easel in the front parlor. And what a history it is: a vanishing guest, two murders, and at least two deaths from cholera or other illnesses since the inn was first built. Is it any wonder that at least three ghosts are said to haunt the inn?

Although Columbian House no longer offers guest rooms, it does still operate as a restaurant, so my wife and I decided to combine our ghosthunting with dinner. When we arrived at six o'clock that evening the place looked dark and closed, but the hand-forged front door latch admitted us inside. I thought I heard a bell ring somewhere inside the inn when we entered, but no one came out to meet us.

We stood in the little front parlor. It was dimly lit compared to the bright August sunshine outside, and it took a few moments before our eyes were adjusted enough to clearly see the fireplace with its dark portrait of a nineteenth-century gentleman hanging above the mantel. In one corner, against the pale blue wall, stood an antique secretary, crammed with old books about Ohio and it's history. An impossibly tall military hat with shako, all in black, stood at attention atop the secretary. A hand-lettered sign described it as a relic of the Toledo War, an 1835 border dispute between the new state of Ohio and the neighboring Michigan

Territory. Bloodshed was averted in the comic opera war because Michigan and Ohio militias wandered hopelessly lost in the swamps of Perry County, Ohio, and could not find each other; Congress ultimately settled the dispute peacefully in Ohio's favor.

A glass-topped wooden display case before the secretary held historic items discovered over the years at the inn. There were pieces of crockery and dinnerware, clay pipes, buttons, thimbles, pins, a knife, part of an Indian moccasin, assorted iron keys, hinges, bolts, and other unidentifiable objects.

Despite the nearness of the road the quiet in the little parlor was thick as dust, broken only by the creaking and groaning of the wooden floorboards beneath our feet. I heard indistinct voices coming from somewhere and ventured into the large dining room off the parlor.

I startled Meredith Parker as she came out of the kitchen.

"Sorry, I didn't hear you come in," she said. "My father told me you were coming. He'll be here a little later to talk with you."

The restaurant was just opening for the evening. Even though Mary and I were the only customers at the time, it was obvious that Meredith was preoccupied with her culinary chores. She did have time to tell us that there were several ghosts at the inn. She had seen one of them often, a little girl wearing a long, old-fashioned white dress.

"Sometimes she'll be in the hall, or I might see her for a moment standing in the doorway," Meredith said. "Objects will disappear and reappear later in odd places, or will move by themselves. I once saw a clothes hanger fly across the room by itself."

As she spoke to us, she kept herself at an odd distance. I wasn't sure if she was simply shy or if perhaps she thought we were ghosts.

She directed us to a sideboard in the dining room and a display of photos taken of customers at the inn. A bluish-white misty shape hovered near the patrons in the photos. As I looked at them I couldn't prove whether or not the shapes were ghosts, but they were clearly anomalies that didn't belong in the photos. One photo showed a smiling couple posing before a fireplace. A small Jack o' lantern sat on the mantel behind the woman just to the right of her head.

"What are we supposed to see in this photo?" Mary asked.

Meredith pointed to the lid of the pumpkin. I noticed it was slightly askew.

"Just as this photo was taken," she said, "the lid flew off the pumpkin and landed on the woman's shoulder. What you are seeing in this photo is the moment when the top lifted off."

I watched Meredith's face as she told us these brief stories. There was nothing in her expression that made me doubt her. In fact, she seemed bored by telling these stories, as if she had told them a hundred times before, and maybe she had. Maybe for her, living with the restless spirits of the dead was nothing unusual.

We still had a few minutes before Meredith was able to seat us, so we roamed through the inn, snapping photos as we went. In addition to the large dining room we now stood in, furnished with old, charmingly scarred tables and chairs, there were other, smaller dining sections adjoining the parlor along the front of the inn.

A narrow staircase, each riser worn and bowed by the footsteps of long departed visitors, led to the second floor. Each step groaned as we headed upstairs.

We came up to a narrow hall. Here, the westering sun flowed into the hall from the windows in the three bedrooms, whose doors all stood open. The sunlight was warm and comforting, but something seemed out of place. A cord strung across each doorway barred us from entering the rooms but allowed us to view the antique furniture and accessories in them.

I turned to the corner bedroom.

A skeleton sat near the doorway.

Seated in a rocker.

Wearing a top hat.

Behind him, a second skull grinned from atop the fireplace mantel.

I thought of the nineteenth-century human ghouls who prowled graveyards, digging up skeletons and fresh cadavers to sell to medical schools. I wondered if these old bones relaxing in the rocking chair had been one of their prize catches. It was strange to think that at one time they had walked, perhaps danced. Did they still dance, rattling in the hall at night?

A crib stood in the corner of the room, a muslin canopy hanging above it. Meredith had said a little girl haunted Columbian House. Was this her crib? Did she still sleep there? Was she there now, peering at us through the bars?

We heard footsteps coming up the stairs.

Tom Parker emerged upon the landing and introduced himself to us.

A Tom Skerritt look-alike, Parker was a man with many interests. He was a successful contractor who was also an avid historian. He had a particular fascination with the history of the old Northwest Territory. Proprietorship of Columbian House was not so much a business venture for him as it was an outlet for his historical interests.

We stood talking in the sunny hall and he told us some of the haunted history of the inn. He pointed to the ladies' room only a few feet from us.

"At one time that used to be a holding cell, used by the sheriff for prisoners in transit, but mostly occupied by the local drunk, who was often locked up there overnight. He'd always complain about being sick and bang on the door to be released. People ignored him, but one time he really was sick. In the morning he was found dead in the cell."

Over the years, former owners and guests of the inn have heard desperate pounding on the door in the middle of the night.

There were more stories.

There was the cholera victim who died while staying at the inn and was hastily buried in a coffin too short for his body, the undertaker breaking the dead man's legs to get the body to fit inside.

There was the guest who vanished from his room shortly after the inn was first opened. Thirty years later a local farmer admitted he had murdered the man—his motivation for murder lost to history—dragged his body down the back stairs, and buried it along the Maumee River. Authorities found the remains exactly where the farmer said they would be.

Suddenly, the sunny hall no longer felt comforting. Then I realized what seemed out of place when we first came up there. The staircase ended on the second floor. Where was the third floor?

John Pray had added the third floor in 1837. It was one huge room with a barrel-vaulted ceiling and was unique for its time. It was a gathering place for people from all around the area and served as a ballroom, reception hall, and political meeting place. It was also the site of a murder. A man attending one such ball was stabbed to death there, perhaps by a rival for the hand of a local lovely. The next morning a maid found the bloodied body in a cloakroom on the third floor. His murderer was never discovered.

I asked Parker about the third floor. He pointed to a solid wood door that was padlocked shut. He said the third floor was only used for storage now and wouldn't let us up to see it. Parker had some other business to attend to, so he let us continue our explorations by ourselves. I took a few more photos of the rooms, and then we headed downstairs for dinner.

We were seated at our table in the dining room, perusing the menu and wondering what tomato pudding, a specialty of the house, tasted like, when Parker came over. I noticed that, just as his daughter had done, he stood at the next table and spoke to us from that distance. There were so many ghost stories about Columbian House, Parker said, that he had set them down on paper. He handed me a copy.

One story from the 1930s relates the experiences of Charles Capron—a former owner of the inn—with noisy ghosts. For several nights he heard footsteps on the stairs and on the second floor, but nobody was ever there. One night, after locking the front doors, he asked his handyman to sleep in one of the second-floor bedrooms. Once again, in the dead of night, the ghostly footsteps were heard walking in the hall. Capron jumped out of bed and threw open his door. At the same time, the handyman, who was also awakened by the sounds, flung open his door. The two men stood blinking at each other from opposite ends of the hall while the invisible guest continued to pace the floor between them. They heard someone descending the stairs and a few moments later heard a loud crashing sound, which Capron was sure came from a large mirror that hung in one of the rooms downstairs. That was too much for the spooked men, who retreated behind their respective doors. In the morning Capron found the mirror to be intact. Nothing was broken or disturbed.

Capron was the man who initially rescued Columbian House from destruction by the wrecker's ball. In the 1920s the inn fell into disrepair and stood derelict for a few years. During that time, the residents of Waterville wanted to tear the building down, ostensibly because it was a safety hazard, but some said the real reason was that the house was evil. Perhaps that was what induced Henry Ford to host a Halloween party there in 1927. In any case, Capron purchased the inn and began restoring it.

The Arnold family, who owned the inn from the 1940s to 1993, reported a "presence" at the foot of the stairs, a strange feeling that something was there. Some of their longtime employees reported the same sensations.

During the Parkers' ownership, several people have heard the sound of a child crying. As Parker was stripping one of the second-floor bedroom's floors of a century's worth of dirt and grime, he uncovered the name "Alice Carroll" painted in a childish hand on the floor. Is little Alice the crying ghost, the ghost that Meredith Parker has seen on several occasions?

"In the years that I've owned the inn, I've never seen anything unusual," Tom Parker said, "but many others have. I'm open to any explanations of what's been going on here for so many years. All I can say is, regardless of any physical evidence, Columbian House has a personality, a character, all its own, obtained from 175 years of use by many people."

Later, when I downloaded the pictures I had taken at Columbian House into my computer, I was surprised to note an anomaly in one photo. The shot was taken from the head of the stairs on the second floor, looking down to the first floor. At the foot of the stairs appeared a small whitish orb of unknown origin. Enlarging the photo did not provide any clues to identifying the orb. I remembered that a member of the Arnold family had been frightened by a "presence" at the foot of the stairs. Was that "presence" now caught in my photo?

Fort Meigs

PERRYSBURG

THERE IS AN AURA OVER A BATTLEFIELD, an aura created by acts of privation, courage, and sacrifice, that cannot be felt at other historical sites. A visitor to such a battlefield can never truly understand the travails of those who fought and died there, but one can feel an emotional tug, a spiritual pang of empathy, at such places. Some say that there is more to that spiritual empathy than we can comprehend and that the spirits of those who have died on the battlefield remain forever bound to it.

Fort Meigs is one of those places.

During the War of 1812, the Northwest Territory was a strategic location and a central area for American military operations.

Until the spring of 1813, the war in the Northwest had gone badly for the Americans. Both Fort Mackinac and Detroit in Michigan Territory were lost to the British and their Indian allies, as well as Fort Dearborn in Illinois Territory. An American defeat on the River Raisin in Michigan was an additional blow to the United States. Only Fort Wayne in Indiana Territory was able to repulse the British attack.

General William Henry Harrison, newly appointed commander of the Northwest Army, was determined to thwart the British advance by establishing a log and earthen fort on a bluff overlooking the southern shore of the Maumee River. The fort was a sprawling structure for its time, built to serve not as a permanent military installation but a temporary supply depot and staging area for an American invasion of Canada. The palisade enclosed ten acres and included seven two-story blockhouses and five artillery batteries. At its greatest strength, approximately two thousand men were sheltered in tents within the fort's perimeter and included U.S. Army regulars, militia from Ohio, Kentucky, Pennsylvania, and Virginia, and several companies of volunteers.

It was difficult to get a sense of that bustling activity on the day I visited the reconstructed fort. I was alone. There was no sound in the vast, open space enclosed by the wooden palisade, other than crickets sawing in the high grass and the wind whispering over the grounds. A solitary hawk floated high above the fort in a sky so hard and blue I felt as though I could reach up and rap it with my knuckles.

As I walked among the traverses—long, earthen berms taller than a man, thrown up as protection against incoming artillery rounds—the wind abated. There was only silence.

It was among these traverses one night that Virginia Pfouts saw the dark shape of a man during a recent Garrison Ghost Walk. Virginia has been a volunteer at Fort Meigs for the last eight years and knows the fort and the other volunteers very well.

"It was more of a silhouette," she said in a conversation after my visit to the fort. "I saw it in an area of the fort that the tour did not visit. There shouldn't have been anyone down there. I got closer and looked down another traverse to where the man had been. He was gone. None of the volunteers said they had been in that section that night. I know it wasn't one of the people on the tour. We count noses and keep a close watch on them so we don't lose anyone in the dark."

During the British sieges of Fort Meigs in May and July, 1813, American observers would stand upon the traverses. By watching how the smoke from British cannons across the river drifted on the wind, they could predict with a fair degree of accuracy where the projectile would hit and shout a warning to the soldiers in that area to duck for cover. It was dangerous work. A solid shot cannon ball could take away a man's head, or leave him standing for a few seconds with a bloody hole big enough to look through drilled through his chest. A "bomb bursting in air," as Francis Scott Key wrote during the same war, could pepper him with shrapnel or turn him into a human torch with flammable resins.

Could Virginia's specter be the ghost of one of these unfortunate casualties?

"Some people have seen ghostly figures walking upon the traverses," said John Destatte, a volunteer with more than thirteen years' experience. "There are certainly enough tragic stories from the fort's past that could account for the many ghost stories."

John told me how a detachment of Kentucky militia came to the aid of the besieged fort, captured a British gun battery across the river, and then fell into a trap set by "retreating" Indians. Those who were not killed in battle were taken prisoner by the Indians and subjected to torture until Shawnee Chief Tecumseh heard about it and put a halt to the tortures, all the while upbraiding the British officers who stood by and let it happen as "women." Of the 800-man detachment, 650 were killed or captured.

"One of them was a captain," John said, "who had been seriously wounded by a musket ball that entered one temple and passed out through the other without killing him. The ball severed his optic nerve and the man was blinded. He wandered over the battlefield until the Indians killed and scalped him."

Indians are said to haunt the fort in addition to the ghostly soldiers. Unbeknownst to General Harrison, the site had been previously used by Native Americans for several centuries. As American soldiers constructed the fort, human remains were unearthed. An entry from the 1813 diary of Captain Daniel Cushing reads:

> In almost every place where we have thrown up the earth we find human bones aplenty. Yesterday the fatigue party that were digging a trench in front of blockhouse No. 3 and 4 came upon a pile of bones where they took out 25 skulls in one pit ... In walking around this garrison on the earth that has been thrown up it was like walking on the sea shore upon mussel shells, only in this case human bones.

It came as no surprise to hear both John and Virginia say that the area around blockhouse No. 3 is where most people report unusual events. John talked about the woman and child sometimes seen peering from a second-floor window, and about the bluish-white light that has been seen floating in the dark near the blockhouse and then drifting down the slope to the river.

"People who have seen it say that it is an Indian spirit, although they can't explain why they feel that way," John said.

Virginia has seen the light.

"It was as bright as a camera flash," she said, "only it lasted longer. A full four seconds, at least. It wasn't a camera. No one in our group was using one. There were no other lights that could have made the flash."

Virginia has had other experiences at blockhouse No. 3. One night, after she and some other volunteers had locked up the blockhouses and were returning to their cars in the parking lot, two police cruisers pulled up. The officers told her that the motion detectors in one of the blockhouses had been triggered. Something was inside.

"Sometimes there will be a false alarm," Virginia said. "Maybe a mouse or something. I went back into the fort to check. The policemen didn't come with me."

She went to all the blockhouses, checked the locks, and found them all securely fastened. Then she came to blockhouse No. 3, with the steep traverse running close before it.

"I was standing at the door in the dark. I checked the lock. It was still locked. Suddenly, I heard the sound of a musket misfiring behind me, from up above the traverse. I whirled around but there was no one there."

"A musket?" I asked.

"I've heard that sound plenty of times during re-enactments. I recognized it immediately."

Are the spirits of Fort Meigs still at war?

John said that some people have seen soldiers firing weapons. Virginia said that two women from Canada saw a ghostly gun crew working a cannon at the fort's Grand Battery at three o'clock in the morning. I never did find out what the women were doing at the fort in the middle of the night, since Virginia did not feel that she should speak on their behalf and no one could remember their full names or where they lived. Canada's a big country.

I didn't see any ghosts at Fort Meigs, but I did find the melancholy gravestones of three officers killed there. The graves were not far from the soaring obelisk that memorializes the soldiers of Fort Meigs. Nor are they far from the cold spot—"refrigerator cold," Virginia called it—that some people have felt even in the brightest sunlight. Indians murdered one of the officers outside the fort. British artillery killed another as he conferred with General Harrison inside the fort, and the other, wounded at the Grand Battery, died from tetanus a few days later. Scores of the dead are buried in unmarked graves just outside the fort's main gate, while others lie in peace in an adjacent cemetery.

During the May 1813 siege, British troops managed to set up an artillery battery on the site now occupied by that cemetery. In a bloody attack, American troops overran the battery and knocked it out of commission. Apparently, that engagement rages on almost two hundred years later. People have heard the sounds of battle—fifes and drums, hoof beats—echoing from the site.

Virginia has heard a soldier walking beside her.

One evening she and some of the other volunteers were walking out from the visitors' center to their cars. Virginia had parked her car in an area removed from the others, and one of the volunteers asked her if she wanted to be escorted to her car. She said no, she had her soldier walking beside her.

"Now, why in the world did I say that?" Virginia said. "It just came out. It was very strange. As I was walking to my car, I had the sense of someone else with me and I heard a little metallic jingling accompanying me. It sounded like the rattling of a musket tool against a belt buckle. Whenever I stopped, the sound stopped, too."

Virginia said she checked her haversack and her camera case, shaking them to see if they were making the sound. They were not. Some time later, another volunteer said she had heard the same sound, only in a different part of the fort.

Virginia had felt the presence of an unseen person before. Once, when she was whitewashing the interior of blockhouse

No. 1, she experienced an overwhelming sensation that some-one was behind her, watching her. She turned to look, but there was no one there. Although she has never heard them herself, Virginia says that some people have heard footsteps pacing the second floor of the blockhouse.

"None of this bothers me," she said. "There is nothing I fear at the fort."

But there are volunteers who refuse to go to certain places within the fort after dark.

"In all my years here," John said, "I have never experienced anything unusual. Yet, people will tell me what they have felt or seen in a certain area of the fort, and I'll research what hap-pened there and say, 'That makes sense.'"

Both John and Virginia are longtime residents of the area and have a long association with Fort Meigs, beginning even before their volunteer days. John, a Perrysburg resident all his life, remembers playing on the traverses as a boy before the fort was reconstructed. Virginia grew up in a house on the site of the Kentucky militia's defeat. They are both sincerely commit-ted to preserving the history and the memory of the fort and its soldiers.

"It really bugs me when people make up stories about what they've seen or heard at the fort," Virginia said. "It makes it so much harder for those of us who have really experienced these things to be believed.

"I believe the spirits of 1813 are still at the fort. It *is* paranor-mal. I don't know how else to explain it."

Indeed.

Ludwig Mill

GRAND RAPIDS

SOME PEOPLE NEVER REALLY RETIRE FROM THEIR JOBS. It is difficult for them to accept the fact that, after being on the job for years and years, their services are no longer required. With no other activities to fall back on they work vicariously, gleaning the latest gossip from the guys down at the plant, listening for the familiar noonday whistle to blow, or watching Engine No. 8 roll through the crossing every afternoon precisely at three o'clock, just as it did when they were on the job.

Perhaps these people return to work in the afterlife. Maybe some of them have come back to Ludwig Mill.

I experienced a vision straight out of the nineteenth century the day Mary and I visited Ludwig Mill in Grand Rapids, along the Maumee River. The *Volunteer,* a blunt-nosed canal boat, was making its slow progress through the massive stone Lock 44 of the canal adjacent to the mill. A tandem team of dusty mules walked the towpath, straining at the line tethering them to the boat, long ears twitching off bothersome flies. A young woman in a bonnet and ankle-length gingham dress stood upon the flat roof of the boat's cabin, over the bow, watching out for obstacles in the narrow canal. Every so often she would turn around to sass a young man in suspenders and a straw hat who stood in the stern complaining loudly in a German-accented voice that canal boating was no kind of work for a woman.

It was 1846 all over again, the year Isaac Ludwig constructed his mill between the bank of the Maumee River and the mosquito-filled trench known as the Miami and Erie Canal.

But it wasn't really 1846, as the arrival of two men in a golf cart filled with sacks of flour proved. We watched the canal boat and its crew of young re-enactors drift out of sight.

The Ludwig Mill and the canal operation are all that is left of the town of Providence, a once bustling and brawling little nineteenth-century burg that was wiped out by fire and cholera. Ludwig Mill is the last of hundreds of mills that once lined the endless miles of canals snaking throughout Ohio, connecting Lake Erie with the Ohio and, eventually, Mississippi rivers and linking distant points within the state through numerous cross canals. The mill is still in operation, using waterpower to mill lumber and grain. Along with the reconstructed Lock 44 and a mile of canal, the mill comprises the Providence Metropark on US24, a mile east of SR578.

The mill itself is an imposing sight, standing tall alongside the river, the Prussian blue clapboards and black metal roof partly shaded by a stand of hickories at the river's edge. At one end of the mill a squarish cupola soars above the trees, the name Ludwig Mill proudly emblazoned in black letters across one side.

It was gloomy inside the mill, and cool. We were the only visitors, our footsteps echoing on the worn wooden floorboards. The interior of the mill was dotted with thick wooden support posts, worn smooth over the years. Hand-hewn beams ran overhead. I saw a set of stairs and catwalks zigzagging back and forth above us, climbing through the upper levels of the mill. The antique framework surrounding us made me feel like Jonah caged in by whale ribs.

There was equipment everywhere, great hulking machines, most of which I could not identify, standing like silent beasts in the dusty air. I did recognize a buzz saw, just like the kind you would see in a Roadrunner and Wyle E. Coyote cartoon, and a large millstone for grinding corn and other grain.

I heard water running somewhere beneath us. We followed the sound and descended into the lower depths of the mill. There we stood upon an iron grate, watching the river rushing below our feet. It was a strong current, but even so, it was difficult to believe that it could generate enough power to run the saws and grinding wheels above us.

We came back up and, while Mary explored one section of the mill, I stepped into the mill office. A wooden rail with a swinging gate separated the business end of the office from the tiny reception area. Just beyond the railing stood a pot-bellied stove, a small table, a couple of wood file cabinets, and a beautiful roll-top desk. Framed black-and-white photos of the mill and various strangers hung on the wall near the door.

"Good morning."

The disembodied voice startled me until I noticed the person sitting in the desk chair, now pushed back from behind the desk so I could see her.

"Hello," I said.

She was a young woman, short and sturdily built. She wore dark woolen pants with suspenders and a blue work shirt. Her hair was tucked up under a floppy mill hat, the kind old-time newsboys used to wear. Her name was Becki Braley, and despite her sudden appearance, she was not a ghost. She was a mill technician and she knew how to operate all the equipment in the mill. I was duly impressed, as I had only recently learned how to program my VCR.

Becki told me she had always been interested in history, especially industrial history, so working as a volunteer at the mill was right up her alley. She showed me around the mill, pointing out various machines and explaining how they worked. Mary met up with us.

My wife is not a professional ghosthunter. She is, in fact, an expert and consultant in the field of occupational safety and health, so she listened intently to Becki's patter.

"Any gruesome deaths?" Mary asked.

"Gruesome deaths?" Becki said.

"You know, anyone pulled into the buzz saw, drowned in the millrace, crushed under a millstone?"

I love it when she talks shop.

Becki said no. The only casualties she knew of were workers getting sawdust in their eyes. I had to admit that could be irritating.

"So no ghosts, then," I said.

"I didn't say that," said Becki. "I've seen a ghost here, and so has another girl. One day I was working in the mill alone. I was standing right over there," she said, pointing to a tight space in front of an old boiler or generator or something. I didn't know what it was, but it was big.

"I heard footsteps and someone walking behind me," she said. "I turned, surprised because no one else was here, and caught a glimpse of a large man wearing old-fashioned work clothes. Dark pants with suspenders, light-colored shirt, and a straw hat. Then he was gone. I went outside and checked with the canal boat people to see if any one of them had been in the mill. They hadn't, nor had any of them seen the man."

"Who do you think it was?" I asked.

Becki led us back into the office and leafed through a history of the mill written by a local historian.

"I'm not certain," Becki said, "but I have a feeling it was Frank Heising."

She showed us a photo of Heising in the book. He was a large man with a big square face.

"He managed the mill from 1919 to 1937. He stood over six feet tall, weighed 250 pounds, and was able to lift a 125-pound bag of grain three feet off the ground with one hand. That's why I think it was him. The guy I saw was a big man."

"What about the other ghost?" Mary asked.

"That was different," Becki said. "It was a child, a little boy most likely. My friend, who was working alone, said she heard footsteps and saw little legs wearing knee-high stockings and knickers run up the stairs. Thinking he was the child of a tourist, she went up the stairs to make sure the boy was okay, but there was no one there. Just as in my story, no one else had seen the child."

Becki wasn't certain, but she thought that Frank Heising had had a son. Were both of them still busy working at Ludwig Mill? Like ghost father, like ghost son?

Northeast

Ashtabula County District Library

ASHTABULA

COULD THERE BE A BETTER PLACE FOR A NEW GHOST
TO LEARN HOW TO BEHAVE as a ghost than a library?
Think of all the books on ghosts and the supernatural just waiting there for the inquisitive spirit's perusal. And their books are
never overdue, checked out for eternity.

The Ashtabula County District Library is built in the grand
architectural style typical of libraries built in the early 1900s. Tall
Corinthian columns support a pointed pediment roof. Long windows flank the columns. The structure sits well back from the
street, separated from it by a neatly trimmed lawn. It is clear that
when the library was built in 1903 it was designed to provide a

quiet place of study, set apart from the hustle and bustle of downtown Ashtabula.

Ashtabula today is a city down at the heels. Not much hustle, even less bustle. The economic downturn that swept through the Midwest's rustbelt did not spare Ashtabula. Still, the library remains in all its grandeur, a symbol of what the past was and, perhaps, of what the future could yet become.

It would please the ghost of Ethel McDowell to know that the library is well maintained and popular. Ethel was the library's first librarian, appointed in 1903. She served in that capacity for sixty-five years, finally retiring in 1968. Ethel retired and passed away, but some say that she never left the building.

In the reference section of the library there is a small room named for McDowell that houses information about Ohio, including a file of newspaper clippings. I thought that it would be a good place to start my research. I was focused on my work as I sat at the desk in the cramped room, looking through files filled with clippings about local cemeteries and historical spots. It was only when I took a break and stretched that I noticed the portrait of Ethel McDowell hanging on the wall behind me. (Note: A ghosthunter really should pay more attention to his surroundings.) Ethel looked like everyone's grandmother (or maybe Barbara Bush)—a chunky woman in a light blue dress, silver horn-rimmed glasses, white hair coiffed in gentle waves. Her mouth was set in an interesting way, almost as if she wanted to smile, but since she was in a library, refusing to do so, favoring instead the stern expression reserved for those young boys who gawked at bare-breasted tribal women in *National Geographic*.

I had the distinct impression that Ethel ran the library with an iron hand.

"Some of the older employees say she is still around," said Diane*, "but I've never seen her." We were standing at the counter in the children's section, located in the basement. Diane told me she had been working there for five years. "I've heard of books falling off the shelves by themselves, and that may not sound like much of anything, but I mean books like these."

She walked over to a shelf that held magazines placed in cardboard holders. "These magazines can't just fall off the shelf," she said. "They actually have to be lifted up out of the holders first, then dropped on the floor. That's what people would find—magazines on the floor, the holders still on the shelf. And there would be no one around."

Although Diane has never claimed to see Ethel's ghost, or any other ghost for that matter, she admits that sometimes she has gotten the feeling that someone has walked by when there was no one there.

As we were talking, Cheryl* came in and stashed a bag she was carrying behind the counter. She overheard our conversation and added that she had heard unexplainable footsteps and other unidentifiable sounds when she was alone, although she thought they could have simply been the typical sounds of a one-hundred-year-old building.

Diane also said that there were stories from before she worked at the library of books being thrown around in the children's section. Of course, the children were immediately reprimanded for such behavior, but they always swore that they had nothing to do with the flying books.

Some of the stories told about the library say that Ethel will toss out the books that she thinks should not be in the library's holdings. Sometimes they will be missing for a while or they will be found scattered on the floor. This seemed to happen more often in the reference section—in fact, in the very room where I had been reviewing the newspaper files.

I went back upstairs to the reference desk and asked Terri*, who had helped me with the files, what she knew about the ghost. She had heard all the stories, as had the other workers, but she did not have any personal experiences to relate. Most of the people who had encountered anything unusual were long gone, she said, which made me wonder if perhaps Ethel herself had finally moved on. After all, wasn't the Celestial Library in need of a steely-eyed librarian to keep things in order?

Although I never did find any true ghost stories in the files, I did find some information about the Ashtabula train disaster of 1876. On the evening of December 29, during a blinding snowstorm, a passenger train carrying 165 passengers plunged into the Ashtabula River gorge when the supports of the bridge spanning the gorge gave way. The train burst into flames when it crashed, fueled by the oil lamps and coal-fired stoves on board. Only sixty people survived.

The *San Francisco Sunday Chronicle* for December 31, 1876, describes the hellish scene: "The charred bodies lay on thick ice or imbedded in the shallow water of the stream. The fires smoldered in great heaps where many hapless victims had all been consumed … of the 165 persons on the train, less than sixty are known to have been saved. The lost are so totally destroyed by fire that it is impossible to identify them. But a few burnt stumps of limbs remain. It is thought that when the creek is dragged a number of bodies will be found."

The unidentified dead were buried in a mass grave in Chestnut Grove Cemetery. There is no trace of the bridge today, but some modern-day ghosthunters have heard unexplainable cries and shouts in the gorge where the train met with disaster.

The Old Tavern

UNIONVILLE

WITH THE EXCEPTION OF THE ELECTRIC UTILITY
LINES RUNNING TO IT and the paved road out front, The
Old Tavern looks unchanged from when it first opened in
1798 as the Webster House inn. The white, saltbox-style building stands sentinel at an intersection in Unionville, diagonally
across from an old cemetery. The four pillars, added in 1820,
give the tavern something of a Mount Vernon look. It is said
that they were added for the benefit of the Marquis de Lafayette,
who had been greatly impressed by George Washington's home
in Virginia and was passing through the area on his way to
Boston for the laying of the Bunker Hill monument. If Lafayette;

or Spencer Shears, the original proprietor of the tavern; or the nineteenth-century settlers heading west in their Conestoga wagons; or the soldiers of 1812 marching to the front; or the drovers herding cattle; or the weary stagecoach passengers traveling the Cleveland-Buffalo road; or the circuit court riders; or the runaway slaves fleeing to freedom via the Underground Railroad; could all return again to the inn, they would feel right at home.

Maybe that's why some of them have returned. Or, perhaps, never left.

Crystal Ketron waited on us the day my wife and I stopped by The Old Tavern. We were acting on a tip we had gotten from one of the librarians in Ashtabula, who told us about the Canterbury Feast Murder Mystery event that the inn held regularly. The librarian said she had also heard stories about the inn being haunted, although she could offer no specific details. That was good enough for us. As Crystal filled our water glasses I asked her right away to tell me about the ghosts. I had found that such a direct approach would either earn me a look that clearly implies I'm crazy, or else the person would open up immediately, wondering how in the world I knew about them. Was I psychic?

I hit pay dirt with Crystal.

Mary and I were seated at a table in a large solarium-like room that was a later addition to the inn. We were overlooking the garden, at this time of year just beginning to show signs of life. It was late on a weekday afternoon. The only other customers in the inn were a group of blue-haired local ladies playing bridge beside a crackling fire in the next room, so Crystal had time to talk with us.

Even though she had only been working at The Old Tavern for less than a year, she had seen and heard a lot.

"Most of what I have experienced has been in the ballroom upstairs," Crystal said. "A couple died in a fire up there many years ago, and now there's an area, sort of an oval, in the middle of the floor where crazy things happen. There was a chair standing there all by itself when, for no reason, it just fell over. Things will always fall over or get knocked around in that spot."

I could imagine the ghostly ballroom dancers knocking into the furniture that wouldn't have been there in their own time and wondering what they had hit.

Crystal also said that she saw wine glasses slide off a hanging rack in the ballroom and crash to the floor, without anyone being around.

"And there's the Crying Lady in the Webster Room, too," she said, warming up to her role as tavern historian. "She was having an affair and when her husband found out, he came here and shot her and her lover dead."

I thought about those ghosts while working through my salad and the corn fritter—originally called a dodger—appetizer served in maple syrup, a specialty of the house, and wondered what else might still be there. After all, The Old Tavern is the oldest tavern in continuous operation in Ohio. Its rooms would have witnessed much of the sorrows and misfortunes of the human condition over the centuries. No doubt those memories still lingered there, ingrained in its very walls.

When Crystal came back from the kitchen with our entrees she told us about some of the strange sounds she and others have heard in the tavern.

"In the basement you can sometimes hear a harmonica playing. I don't know anyone who has seen him, but some people get a strong feeling that there is a little boy down there. The story goes that the boy was abandoned at the tavern and the owner let him stay there, doing odd jobs in return for food and shelter.

"Once, at Christmas, another waitress and myself heard Christmas carols playing and we didn't know where they were coming from. Even with our own sound system turned way up we still heard them," she said.

It's not only human spirits who wander the tavern. Crystal told us about Diane, another waitress, and her brush with a ghost cat. Diane was working in the kitchen when she felt something brush against her feet. She looked down and was startled to see her shoelaces untying themselves. It wasn't that they had already become untied; they were actually unknotting themselves before her very eyes. Another time, in order to test her ghost cat hypothesis, Diane crumpled a piece of paper into a ball—a great cat toy—tossed it casually on the floor, and left the room. When she returned awhile later she couldn't find the paper ball anywhere. She finally found it on a counter in another room, wet and slobbered.

A ghost cat? Apparently so. Ghost literature is full of stories about animal spirits, especially cats. That makes sense; with nine lives a cat can make a hell of a lot of ghosts.

After lunch, Crystal said we could explore the tavern. From the porch dining room we stepped into a smaller dining room at the back of the inn. It was gloomy in there since it was not being used and most of the lights were off. The walls were painted light blue and were also papered in an old-fashioned quilt design. The ceiling was so low in this old part of the tavern that I could reach up and touch it without fully extending my arm—and I am not a particularly tall man.

A large mirror in an ornate gilt frame hung above the mantel over the fireplace. A colorful Easter basket filled with pastel-colored eggs sat on the mantelpiece. I approached the mirror, which reflected little besides the basket directly before it because of the darkness of the room. Some psychic researchers believe that mirrors, in some unexplainable manner, can act as conduits, called portals, between the spirit world and this world. Only a few days before, when Mary and I had stayed at

Rider's Inn in Painesville, the owner had told us how a huge crack had suddenly opened up in the wall of a room when a mirror owned by a long-dead mistress of the inn was discovered and hung on the wall. As I thought about that, I recalled the old tradition of covering mirrors with black cloth when someone in the house passed away. What inspired that tradition? Was the cloth supposed to block the portal, thereby preventing the spirit from returning to the living?

Crystal had told us that the mirror in that room was a portal for the ghosts roaming the tavern. I stood before it in the gloom, peering into its depths, trying to see beyond something I could not see. I had the weird sensation that I was standing in a flood of psychic energy. Were ghosts even now passing back and forth through this portal, coming and going like the old-time stagecoach passengers who streamed through the tavern so long ago? I took a picture of the mirror with no expectations of capturing anything. Later, when I downloaded the image into my computer, I noticed some whitish streaks in the mirror that I could not explain, but to be objective, flash photography on a reflective surface in low light could be the cause of the "ghost" in the image. Then again, maybe not.

Mary and I went upstairs to the second floor. We had the upstairs floor entirely to ourselves, since none of the rooms were in use and the tavern no longer offers overnight accommodations. The stairs were carpeted in an autumnal leaf motif. Gold patterned wallpaper adorned the walls, and a reproduction glass gas lamp hung suspended above the stairs.

The first room we entered was the ballroom. It was a large wood-floored room with a row of windows that looked out over the street. The first thing I noticed as I walked around in the room was that the old floor was uneven and warped. I felt like I was onboard a boat in a rolling sea. The boards creaked as I stepped on them. Even though the floor was uneven, however, I didn't think that would explain a chair falling over by itself. The room was decorated in a medieval theme for the Canterbury Murder Mystery, with colorful flags and pennants hanging from the ceiling. Two wooden thrones sat on a dais at one end of the room. The festive décor effectively masked any sense of the tragic fire Crystal had spoken about.

Across the hall from the ballroom was the Webster Room. This was a small dining room designed for private occasions with a half-dozen or so tables. The room, which was papered in a cream-colored pattern and was much lighter than the ballroom, originally served as sleeping quarters for road-weary guests. A woman's straw sunhat, bedecked with yellow flowers and blue ribbons, hung upon the door to the room and gave it a false sense of gaiety, since it was in the Webster Room that the enraged husband shot his wife and her lover. The mournful sobs of the Crying Lady can still be heard in the Webster Room, although the day that I visited she was quiet.

While Mary continued to poke around on the second floor, I discovered a staircase to another floor above. Unlike the stairs to the second floor, these stairs were narrow, the walls plain and unadorned of any decoration. A simple iron handrail ran up one side, but what attracted me most was the comical ghost decal stuck over the light switch at the foot of the stairs. If ever there was a sign from the spirit world for me, that was it. I went upstairs.

From the first creaking step, I began to experience an odd, disturbing feeling, a sort of anxiety. I felt heavy, leaden, and by the time I reached the top of the stairs, it felt as though I was pushing through an invisible wall thick as molasses.

None of the floors up here were carpeted, and my footsteps echoed on the wide planks of the old wood floors. There was a room to my right, which I entered. I first came into a tiny anteroom. A large old chest lay on the floor. In a long open closet off that room hung vintage clothes. I crossed the anteroom and came into a corner room with an eclectic mix of furniture that seemed both old and modern at the same time. In this room was a battered old cupboard with some oil lamps standing on it; a sickly green plush easy chair, circa 1970; an oval braided rug; a side table with porcelain washbasin and pitcher; and an antique metal bathtub, a narrow, coffin-like contraption.

A half-wall separated the room from another just beyond it that contained a single bed in a wooden cannonball bed frame with a modern mattress upon it, no sheets; an old dresser; and a few strange odds and ends—a doll, a small oil painting of a woman, a pair of candlesticks.

I stood there between the two rooms, trying to make sense of the feelings washing over me. Despite the fact that light came in through the windows and the walls were painted a very pale green, it still seemed oppressively dark and depressing in there. My attention was focused mostly on that first room, and I had the distinct impression that someone was there, or had been there recently. Something about the coverlet thrown casually over the arm of the green chair made me think that it had just been in use, but by whom? And why? Those rooms were not exactly comfortable and I could see no reason why anyone would want to spend any time in them. As strange as the chair made me feel, there was something worse about the tub. Was it simply that it resembled a coffin, or was there something more?

The room was weighing down on me. I wanted to see if Mary felt the same thing, so I called downstairs for her to come up. She came up and entered the room. The first thing she noticed was the bathtub.

"What's that?" she said. "It looks like a coffin."

"A bathtub."

"I couldn't imagine taking a bath in that," Mary said, "it creeps me out just looking at it."

Bingo.

Mary is a scientist, one not easily impressed by "feelings" or "sensations," one not easily "creeped out," but there was something at work in that room that even got to her. We didn't stay there much longer.

As we left the room and stood at the top of the stairs, Mary opened a door across from the room we had just left. It revealed an unfinished attic, piled high with assorted junk. We went back down to the first floor.

There is a gift shop on the first floor and I bought a book that talked about the history of The Old Tavern. In the book is a photograph of a blond-haired little boy sitting on a bench in the basement. Along the wall to his left are rows of canned and preserved foods arranged on shelves. He sits in the corner of the basement, the stones of the foundation wall behind him. He is wearing something like a jumper and his skinny little arms and legs are bare. His hands are folded in his lap and he looks directly at the camera with a calm and angelic face. The caption below the photo says the boy is unidentified. I wondered if he played the harmonica.

I also read in the book that the runaway slaves who stopped at The Old Tavern on their long journey to freedom in Canada not only used the tunnels carved out of the basement, but also a loft space accessed by "secret stairs." Could the escaped slaves have used those upstairs rooms that seemed so foreboding to me? Are their spirits still there today?

Main Street Café

MEDINA

IT BEGAN WITH HOT WATER SUDDENLY GUSHING FROM THE FAUCETS AT NIGHT, unexplainable rushes of cold wind, and exploding light bulbs, but Psychic Sonya knew beyond any doubt that the Main Street Café on the Medina town square was haunted when she received the impression of a man sitting on the stairs, watching her do a Tarot card reading.

"I kept seeing the letter D," Sonya said, "and eventually his name came to me: Daniel."

Sonya didn't know why the man was there or what he wanted, until she heard that human bones had been found in the coffee shop next door during a renovation project and that

the owner of the shop had discarded them. I could not understand why the owner would not have notified the police about
finding the bones, but Sonya didn't have an answer for that.

"All I can say is that you never desecrate human remains. It's
a bad thing to do—really bad juju," Sonya said as we talked on
the phone.

I had been to the Main Street Café only a few weeks before,
but was unable to meet with Sonya at that time. The building
that houses the restaurant is 120 years old. Behind the purple
and blue façade and the frosted glass windows, the décor inside
recreates that old-time feel with high ceilings, ceiling fans, and
wood floors. A handsome old bar and cozy lounge are at the
rear of the main dining room. Halfway across the room is a
staircase that leads to the basement dining room.

It is in the basement where most of the ghostly activity took
place.

The basement was brick-walled with a low ceiling, the beams
exposed. The lighting was dim, provided by only a few small
lamps scattered throughout the room and a couple of spotlights. Half a dozen or so tables draped in white tablecloths
awaited guests. A bar stood at one end of the room. At the
opposite end was a large mural depicting a bearded old man
dressed in eighteenth-century style breeches and shirt,
sprawled on his back, eyes closed, an empty wineglass in his
hand. Floating in the distance was a vineyard. In the foreground,
floating above him, were two naked women sprawled on clouds,
one facing the viewer, the other providing a delectable rear view.
The mural carried a mixed message, both erotic and pathetic at
the same time.

I was alone in the basement. It was cooler down there than it
was upstairs, but that was to be expected in a subterranean setting. No rush of wind. No exploding light bulbs. I glanced over
at the stairs where Sonya had sensed the spirit of Daniel, but

I'm not psychic and didn't feel anything. I took a few pictures then went back upstairs.

One of the waitresses told me about another waitress who had set the tables downstairs, lit all the candles, then left the room. When she came back only a few minutes later, every place setting—every knife, fork, and spoon—had been turned upside down.

Now, three weeks later, Sonya was telling me that things were much worse than that. Daniel was acting up.

"He seemed to be attaching himself to Frank*, the dishwasher, in particular," Sonya said. "Frank used to wear this old Marine compass on a chain around his neck. One day, it suddenly shattered into pieces. He had worn it for years and had never had any problem. Then light bulbs started exploding and Frank cut his hand when he went to change one of them. He was becoming so annoyed by the ghost that at one point, he said he would like to send it back to hell. No sooner had he said that than he fell down the basement stairs, injuring his neck and shoulder."

Sonya brought in two friends to help her get rid of Daniel. One was a psychic investigator, the other, a healer. They set up a video camera and tape recorder. While they did not record any images, they did record an EVP, an electronic voice phenomenon.

"There was nothing but silence on the tape. Then, clear as a bell, a man's voice said, 'Go away.' I knew then that Daniel would not go easily," Sonya said.

Sonya continued her research and put together a plausible story for the spirit of Daniel. She said he came from Cleveland and was only in his twenties when he died, sometime around 1830. She doesn't know how he died, but she is sure he did not receive a proper burial. She believes the bones discovered in the wall next door belonged to Daniel and that his haunting is a result of the desecration exacted upon his final resting place.

I wondered if there might not be another explanation for the ghost. Sonya's research revealed that at one point, the building was home to Longacre & Son Furniture. In days gone by, furniture makers frequently doubled as coffin makers, since they had the tools, materials, and skills to do the job. During a winter cholera epidemic that hit Medina in the mid-nineteenth century, victims were stored in coffins in the building until warmer weather made the ground softer for burial. Couldn't one of those poor unfortunates have been the ghost? Could it be that Daniel himself was a cholera victim?

Sonya said that she was interested in knowing the ghost's history only to the point that it would help her get rid of it. "I don't care what its story is," she said. "It's leaving." She said that ghosts simply do not belong here, and that people who try to live with ghosts are doing both themselves and the spirits a disservice.

"Ghosts are earthbound spirits. They are trapped here when, in fact, they need to move on. They're not healthy to have around, period. They have to go. Some of them don't even know they're dead, but once they understand that, they will move on. Others, like Daniel, are more stubborn and don't want to go," she said.

Sonja was concerned about the dishwasher, Frank. His co-workers were telling her that his personality was changing. He was becoming depressed, sometimes surly and angry. Sonja feared that Daniel was taking over.

With her two friends, Sonja conducted a healing ceremony at the restaurant, which was recorded by a reporter and photographer from a local newspaper. Sonja didn't give me the details, but did say that her team was able to free Frank from the ghost's influence.

After the ceremony, Sonja, the healer, and the photographer went out into the alley near the wall where the bones had been found. There, she knelt in the snow, said the prayers of a Christian burial service, and gave Daniel the rites that had been denied him so long ago. She looked up and saw a huge, bright cloud above the photographer's head.

"It was the angels, come to take Daniel away," she said. "He didn't want to go. I saw him kicking and screaming as the angels dragged him away."

It has been quiet at the Main Street Café since that incident, but are the ghosts really gone? What about all those cholera victims? Are they still around? And what about that shining white orb I discovered I had captured on film, hovering by the basement stairs? What was that? Only time will tell.

Medina Steakhouse & Saloon
MEDINA

**THE SPIRITS LED ME TO MEDINA STEAKHOUSE &
SALOON, I AM CERTAIN.**

Mary and I were headed north, on our way to more ghost-hunting adventures in Cleveland, when we developed car trouble just outside of Akron. I managed to pull off into a golf driving range and pro shop, where we waited more than three hours for a AAA wrecker to finally tow us to the repair shop only twelve miles away. While we waited for the wrecker I chatted with the manager of the pro shop. He told me about a haunted restaurant in nearby Medina that had been the recent subject of a newspaper article. He could not remember the name of the restaurant, however.

The next day, with the aid of a loaner car from the repair shop, we drove into Medina. I stopped at the library and was surprised to find a "ghost file" containing clippings about Ohio hauntings. In that file I found the newspaper accounts the golf manager had mentioned. They were about the Main Street Café, but in another clipping there was a brief mention of the haunting of the Medina Steakhouse & Saloon.

It turned out that the repairs my car needed were minor and easily accomplished. What at first was an inconvenience ended up being really nothing at all, but the breakdown and delay provided two new locations for me to explore. Maybe the Medina ghosts had joined forces to get me to stop and say hello.

The Medina Steakhouse & Saloon looks like something right out of the 1890s. The two-story former stagecoach stop is an imposing yet inviting structure. Six slender columns graced the front of the red-and-white facade. On the second floor, a wide verandah wrapped around two sides of the restaurant. A red hip roof topped the building.

Large glass windows lined the front of the building, flanking red double doors with etched glass windows. Above the larger windows the restaurant's offerings were proudly spelled out in fancy gold letters: steaks, seafood, ribs and chops, beer, cigars, and spirits. It was the last one, of course, that caught my eye. This place actually advertised its ghosts.

Inside, everything was made of deep, rich mahogany accented by bright brass fixtures. Old framed photos hung on the mahogany-paneled walls. Ceiling fans gently cut the air. There was a fine old mahogany bar in the room next to the one in which we were seated. It was still Ohio, but the decor made me think that Wyatt Earp or Buffalo Bill Cody could walk through the front doors at any moment.

But there was enough Ohio history there to fill a few books and provide for a posse of ghosts, as well. Built in 1858, the

Medina Steakhouse & Saloon was originally a stagecoach stop. Travelers could book rooms upstairs for the evening, and it's likely those same rooms may have been booked by the hour by ladies of the evening who plied their trade there. Although it hasn't been documented, it is possible that the inn also served as a station on the Underground Railroad, as did so many public houses in Northeast Ohio.

Deciding not to beat around the bush, I told our waitress I had read an old newspaper article describing how the owner of the restaurant had succeeded in contacting the spirit of a woman named Anna. I asked her if I could talk to the owner about her ghost.

"She's long gone," said Nancy, our waitress. "There've been three or four owners since then."

"I wonder if the ghosts are gone, too," I said.

"Oh no, we still have ghosts," Nancy said, "but they're not bad. We're used to them."

Nancy Lengel was a pleasant, middle-aged woman who had worked at the restaurant for six years. Two young girls in server uniforms of white blouses and black pants were following her very closely. So closely, in fact, that every time she turned around she would bump into them. Their eyes grew large when Nancy talked about the ghosts.

"It looks like you've got two ghosts of your own shadowing you," I said.

She laughed and explained that the girls, one of them her daughter, were seventh-graders and that she was, indeed, being shadowed by them for a school project. "One of those go-to-work-with-your-parents kind of thing," she said.

I could imagine what stories her daughter would be telling at school the next day: "First I helped my mom fill the water glasses, then I served the salads for some wacky writer guy and his wife, then we all went on a hunt for the ghost of the man who hanged himself upstairs."

Just another day at the Medina Steakhouse.

The article I had found said that Marcelle Arndt, a former owner of the restaurant who also identified herself as a parapsychologist, had contacted Anna through a session with a Ouija board. Anna told her that she had died in the inn in 1895. Anna's connection to the inn wasn't clear. Was she a former innkeeper? Part of the staff? No one knows, but she seemed to care very much for the inn, as though she had invested much of her time and energy into it while she was alive. Apparently, she continued to do so after she died. The article recounted how a fire had broken out in a room on the second floor. The old building had no sprinkler system, and such a fire could have been catastrophic. But even before the firemen could arrive, the fire somehow put itself out, causing only minimal damage confined to a small area. Marcelle was convinced that Anna saved the inn from destruction.

"Do you know about the fire?" I asked Nancy.

"Yes, it was put out by our ghost, Ann."

"Anna?"

"We call her Ann," she said. "If you would like, I could show you where it happened after you've finished your dinner."

Mary and I decided to take her up on her offer.

The newspaper account also mentioned that Marcelle had contacted a second spirit, the ghost of a man who had hanged himself in the upstairs hallway. I asked Nancy about that as she cleared away our plates, her two young assistants dutifully trailing behind.

"There is a male ghost here, too," she said. "Rose and I were both here when the psychic contacted him."

"Psychic?"

"The owner brought in a psychic to try and get rid of the ghosts, but it didn't work."

"A ghostbuster," said Rose, who had come over to our table to join in the conversation. "We did learn the names of our ghosts."

Rose had worked at the restaurant for eighteen years. Thin and energetic, she popped in and out of our conversation while she went about her chores, speaking of the ghosts as if they were everyday occurrences, which I suppose they were.

"The psychic said the man's name was Frank Curtis and that he was a handyman at the inn who died on Christmas Eve, 1922."

"The Dickens you say," I said.

"What?" Rose asked.

"Never mind, go ahead."

"We actually checked it out at the cemetery," Rose said.

"We found a Frank Curtis in Spring Grove Cemetery," Nancy said, "and the dates matched what the psychic told us."

"But the name was spelled with a double S. C-U-R-T-I-S-S," said Rose.

"It was?" said Nancy.

The women seemed momentarily confused by the spelling of the ghost's name, but they sorted it out. All I knew was that these two women had gone to the cemetery hunting the ghost's grave, and had evidently found it. That was a story in itself, I thought.

"Did you tell him about M?" Rose asked Nancy.

"M is another female ghost here, maybe the sister of Ann. And according to the psychic, she is almost identical in looks to Rose," Nancy said. "She follows Rose everywhere."

"The psychic couldn't get her name, though," said Rose. "All she could get was the first letter, M. We think maybe Mary, Marie, something like that."

Rose ran off again and Nancy told us how the housekeeper had come in one morning and had seen Rose going upstairs. Except it wasn't her; Rose didn't come into work until later. Nancy said that Rose also feels a presence in the car with her when she drives home from work, but that it is a protective spirit and not harmful. Perhaps it is M, making sure her modern-day doppelganger gets home safely.

After dinner, Mary and I went upstairs. The second floor was originally partitioned off into smaller guest rooms, but the most recent configuration eliminated the smaller rooms and created two dining areas that are used for parties and special events. It was quiet there compared to the busy dining room on the first floor, since the rooms were not in use that evening.

I peered into the smaller of the two rooms. The walls were papered in a dull beige color and set off by a paneled wainscot. Half a dozen or so round tables set with white tablecloths and ringed by mahogany straight-backed chairs filled the room. Green window shades were pulled halfway down, and the darkness outside swarmed against the windowpanes. The room was silent now—no trace of the travelers or "gentleman johns" who had frequented them in earlier years.

Nancy and the two girls joined us upstairs. While Mary stood talking with them in the larger of the two dining rooms, I explored a narrow, twisting hallway at the opposite end of the building. It was dark in the hall, which wasn't very long at all once I made the initial turn. A restroom opened to one side, a supply closet on the other. At the end of the hall was a set of stairs that must have led to an attic. Although there was little to see in the hall, I thought that it might be important in explaining the ghostly activity going on at the restaurant, so I stepped back a few feet and took a picture. When I returned to the others Nancy told me that it was in that hall, in the rear toward the attic steps, that a man had hanged himself. A few moments later, I noticed that the two girls were tentatively exploring the hall, holding on to each other, prepared to run at a moment's notice if need be.

Nancy explained that as far as she and her coworkers could tell the ghosts were friendly. Mischievous, yes, but not harmful.

She told us how she had spent some time arranging the place settings on the long banquet table in the larger dining room, only to find them all misplaced when she came back into the room. She told us about the kegs of beer that the chef had seen moving by themselves in the basement, and about the tulip-painted plate resting on a plate rack in the main dining room that would often be found in the morning turned with its painted side facing the wall. She told us that some of the workers there had sensed the presence of a large dog, perhaps a German shepherd, even though there is no dog at the restaurant.

With such a colorful past and three identified ghosts, you might wonder if perhaps there are even more spirits in the restaurant who have not yet made their existence known to us mere mortals. Further investigation might shed more light upon the resident ghosts at the Medina Steakhouse & Saloon.

Rider's Inn

PAINESVILLE

SOME SAY THAT GHOSTS LINGER IN A PLACE THEY
LOVED IN LIFE, a place where they felt their happiest. Their
ghostly existence is tied to that place, and they become its pro-
tectors and otherworldly guardians. The ghost of Suzanne Rider
is one such protective spirit; she has saved Rider's Inn from
destruction several times and has even saved the life of the inn's
owner, Elaine Crane.

We were sitting in Mr. Joseph's English Pub in the inn,
named for Joseph Rider, the man who built the inn in 1812. I
had just finished my spiced apple fruit cup and scrambled eggs
and was lingering over my coffee when Elaine pulled over a

chair and joined me. She straddled it backwards, leaning over the back as she told me how Suzanne saved her life.

"I had only recently purchased the inn and was renovating it," she said. "One day in August I was working in one of the bathrooms trying to remove some old Italian tile from the wall, hoping to use it in another room. Except for my cat, Sasha, I was alone. I'm still not really sure how it happened, but as I was removing the tile the entire wall suddenly collapsed and fell on me, pinning me on my back.

"The tile had sharp edges and I was cut from here to here," Elaine said, drawing her hand diagonally across her chest in a twelve-inch slash. "I was bleeding badly. I felt a tile jabbed into my side and I could feel the blood running down. I was dizzy and growing faint and I could not free myself from under the debris. Then I felt what I thought was the cat brush against my hair and I was finally able to free my right hand and dig myself out. I was covered in blood as I drove myself to the hospital, where they put sixteen stitches in me. I called my husband to pick me up.

"I had lost a lot of blood and was still weak, but I was in a hurry to get back to the inn and clean up the mess before the blood stained the floors. That's what we did, despite my husband's objections. I told him what had happened and how the cat had revived me, in a sense, to free myself. 'What do you mean?' he said. 'The cat wasn't here. Look.' There was not a single print from a cat's paw in the plaster and dust from the wall. There were only the prints from my sandals and, above and around those, the prints from a pair of high-heeled shoes. Of course, there had been no one there with me when the wall fell, and no person had helped me out of the debris."

Elaine was sure Suzanne helped her that day, and I had no reason to doubt her. A retired lawyer and judge and now an independent businesswoman, Elaine is a no-nonsense type of person. If she says a spirit saved her life, I believe her.

In fact, I may have had an encounter of sorts with Suzanne myself.

When my wife, Mary, and I first arrived at Rider's Inn, General Manager Bob Beauvais took us on a tour of the eleven guest rooms, all the while giving us a running commentary on the history of the inn. Bob assumed that, since I was writing a book about ghosts, we would want to stay in room number eleven, Suzanne's room. I didn't know at the time what he meant by that, but that is the room we chose.

Suzanne's room is a quiet room at the back of the inn, accessed by a long, narrow corridor. Inside, the rose-colored floral print curtains matched the wallpaper. A bright brass headboard and footboard accentuated the bed, which was arranged below a ceiling fan. There was an old desk with a comfy side chair beside it, and a side table over which hung an antique mirror. In one corner was an old rocking chair, and behind that a white nightgown hung from a hanger on a coat rack. The nightgown had belonged to Suzanne, as had the side table and mirror.

It was difficult to sleep that night. The room was hot, so I opened two windows to bring in some of the cool March air. Even then, I couldn't sleep. My wife is a light sleeper and is easily startled awake, but normally I sleep like the proverbial log. That night was different. Mary awoke with a start several times, and each time she did, she woke me. I also awoke often on my own. The night air flapped the shades over the windows, and the door rattled in its frame as if someone were trying to get inside. I knew what caused these sounds, but still something didn't seem right. Every now and then I would find myself sitting up in bed, gazing at the nightgown across the room. A light from somewhere outside the window made it glow as it hung there, "floating" in the darkness. A bar of light fell across the rocking chair in front of it, and it almost looked like a figure was sitting there.

This went on throughout the night and I felt uneasy, even though I could not come up with any rational explanation as to why I should feel that way. Sometime around three thirty in the morning, I heard the sound of rushing wind moaning and whistling through the room. It came from the window behind the bed—the only window in the room that was *closed*. The sound was exactly what one would imagine hearing in a winter storm, although there was no storm that night. It lasted for only a few moments and then was gone. That sound caught my attention, since the other windows had been open all night and there had not been any such sound from them. I fell back to sleep again, but was once again awakened, perhaps an hour later, by that same strange sound of blowing wind. This time I noticed that, despite the strength of the wind implied by that sound, nothing was disturbed in the room, nor was I actually able to *feel* the ghost wind.

Morning finally came. It was only after that restless night that I read the journal beside the bed. Other guests in room number eleven, Suzanne's room, had written comments about their stay. The entries began in June 2002, covering a year and a half worth of guest observations. The majority of them simply talked about how enjoyable their visits to this charming old inn were, but half a dozen or so had something else to say. Most of these entries talked about being awoken suddenly throughout the night, especially between three and four o'clock in the morning, when I had heard the wind.

One entry read, "I have been woken up between 3 and 4 A.M. with a startle and I can't explain why. Also, the rocking chair moved in the middle of the night." Another read, "Shelly says she saw the rocking chair moving around 4 A.M. It must have been Suzanne." An entry from July 2003 caught my eye: "I heard in the corner above where the doll sits, toward the ceiling area, an *'Ahhh! Ahhh!'* something like the moan of a woman."

Had that guest heard the same moaning wind I had heard, or had he heard something else?

One couple wrote that they had intentionally come there to find the ghost of Suzanne. They set up a video recorder and wired it to the television, hoping to catch her in real time, but they couldn't get their equipment to work properly.

There were some other interesting entries in the journal to consider, such as this one: "A lot of motion going on in the room, but no ghost if you know what I mean." A little smiley face followed the note.

And I had to wonder about this one: "The ceiling light spun counterclockwise to the fan and later blew out, showering sparks upon the bed. It was a close call, for only moments before I was sprawled upon the bed in my naked glory."

Too much information, I thought.

I can't explain what I felt in Suzanne's room, but the feelings were real enough. Elaine Crane told me that renowned psychic Jean Dixon had once been a guest at Rider's Inn and that she had definitely confirmed the existence of spirits residing there.

"Spirits are unfinished business," Elaine said as we sat in the pub that morning. "If people would open their minds to the fact that we are all energy that is transferred into other forms, they would recognize more spirits among them."

Suzanne's unfinished business is, no doubt, to take care of the inn, since she had so little time to do so in life. Suzanne Hitchcock was once described as "the ugliest woman in Painesville"—harsh criticism, indeed, in a time when most people had bad teeth and didn't bathe regularly. But what Suzanne lacked in looks she made up for in wealth, being the daughter of a wealthy and prosperous man. Joseph Rider, on the other hand, was a man down on his luck. Rider immigrated to Ohio from Connecticut in 1795, had already buried two wives, and was watching the inn he had established in 1812 drift closer to bankruptcy when he married Suzanne in 1834. When people made fun of him for marrying such an ugly woman, Rider said, "Anyone would bring a dog in out of the cold." Yes, especially a rich one.

Six weeks after the couple was married and Suzanne had become mistress of the inn, she died. The newspapers cited the circumstances of her death as "strange and mysterious." Six weeks later, the sorrowful widower buried his grief by marrying for the fourth time, this time to a woman who bore him twins only six months later.

It should come as no surprise then that Suzanne, who died at the inn, would choose to remain for eternity in the place where she had enjoyed her short-lived but, one would hope for her, blissful marriage.

In the years following its establishment as an inn, the building served as a stop on the Underground Railroad, a hospital for returning Civil War soldiers, and a 1920s speakeasy, and at one point was derelict and a hangout for drug dealers. Yet, even with so many colorful characters playing a part in the history of the inn, it seems that Suzanne is the one with staying power.

"She looks out for us," Elaine said. "She takes care of the inn."

She told me about the night she received a call from a man who cancelled the reservations that had been made for a couple that night at the inn. Since there were no other guests at the inn that night, Elaine and her staff went home. The following morning, one of Elaine's maintenance workers called her at home and asked her who was in room number six, since the door was locked. Elaine told him there should be no guests at the inn and hurried over to find out what was going on.

When Elaine got to the inn, she knocked on the door of number six and identified herself as the innkeeper. To her surprise, a young man opened the door. Before Elaine could say a word, he began to berate her for her rudeness the previous evening. He thought her behavior was inexcusable. Why had she opened the door without saying a word to the couple—newlyweds, it turned out—and merely pointed to the stairs? Why had she greeted them in her nightgown?

Elaine was stunned. Of course, she had not been the one to let them in, but then who did? She made some apology to mollify the angry man, but she remained confused. Later, she found out that the groom's best man had cancelled the couple's reservation as a joke. Luckily, Suzanne's spirit was still on the job and let the couple in. Elaine said that other guests have also been admitted to the locked inn after hours when she was not around and that their hostess matches the description of Suzanne.

There have been other incidents, as well, in which Suzanne has looked over the welfare of the building itself. One night Elaine awoke and saw a candle lit in one of the rooms. A friend staying at the inn awoke at the same time and saw the same candle burning. As they went to put it out, they heard the sound of running water coming from downstairs. When they went downstairs to investigate, the sound was louder. They realized it was coming from the basement. There they found that the water heater had broken, flooding the basement and threatening the inn's electrical equipment. They were able to turn off the water and prevent any further damage.

Another time, a man who stayed at the inn regularly on business trips—and was treated more as a member of the family than as a guest—was sitting up late in the pub watching a James Bond marathon on television. As she was retiring upstairs for bed, Elaine reminded him to turn off the coffee pot on the kitchen stove when he was finished. He assured her he would. The next morning when Elaine came downstairs, she found the exterior door to the kitchen wide open, letting in rain and snow during the night. Elaine was angry at first, until she noticed the partly melted coffeepot still on the stove. Had the door not opened during the night and extinguished the smoldering pot, the inn could have caught fire. The guest was apologetic about forgetting to turn off the stove but swore that the door had been securely locked when he finally went to bed. No one else had been down in the kitchen overnight.

No one else, that is, except Suzanne, the mistress of Rider's Inn.

Warehouse on the Canal
CANAL FULTON

IF I WERE A GHOST, I'D WANT TO HAUNT THE WARE-HOUSE ON THE CANAL, an old three-story brick building that has been renovated and now houses an antique store, a few art galleries, a doll hospital, a hair salon, the Let's Mango Tea Garden Restaurant, and, of course, a host of friendly spirits. I'd want to haunt it because Ken and Margarita Roberts, who own the building and operate the restaurant, are quite welcoming of their ghosts, and Sherri Brake-Recco, a registered ghosthunter who lives in town, conducts frequent ghosthunting dinners in the warehouse. A spirit would never be lonely for friendly human companionship here.

Canal Fulton is one of those little Ohio towns that developed along the thousands of miles of canals hand-built across the state in the early nineteenth century. Scots-Irish immigrants did most of the work, back-breaking labor complicated by whisky, accidents, and diseases such as dysentery, typhoid, and malaria, also known as "canal fever." So many laborers died building the canals that they were simply and quickly buried in hastily dug graves beside the trenches or in nearby paupers' cemeteries. It is said that for every mile of canal an Irishman is buried, and Canal Fulton may have more than its share of dead Irishmen.

The advent of the railroad heralded the end of the canals, and with their demise came the decline of canal towns like Canal Fulton. But for the Finnifrock family, business was always good. In 1906 they built a new three-story building on North Canal Street to house their furniture-making business. Finnifrock's Fine Furniture was especially known for its bridal suites for newlyweds, but was also known for less hopeful pieces of carpentry: coffins. From 1916–1936, the basement was used as a mortuary. Later, in the 1980s, the pieces of broken headstones from the town's Pioneer Cemetery were stored in the then-empty warehouse. All this goes a long way toward explaining the spiritual energy that Sherri Brake-Recco can detect with her electromagnetic frequency (EMF) meter, remote thermometer, digital camera, and divining rods.

"Divining rods?" I asked her during my visit to the warehouse. I was sitting with her at a little table in Let's Mango. "You mean like some people use to find water?"

With her red hair and blue eyes, Sherri looks every inch the quintessential Irish Colleen, and she assured me that her Celtic heritage plays a part in her abilities to detect paranormal energies.

"You can use them to detect human energy as well," she said. "You can find unmarked graves and even detect the sex of the person who is buried there by using divining rods."

"Have you detected anything here?"

"Yes, in many places in the warehouse, especially the basement where the mortuary used to be."

Diving rods, or dowsing rods, have been used for thousands of years by people all around the globe to find water (think Moses striking the rock with his rod and water gushing forth). Somehow, and no one really knows exactly how, the rods are sensitive to energy sources and are today used by many people, including electrical utility workers who use them to find underground electrical lines, and ghosthunters who zero in on the electrical energy emanating from dead bodies or lively spirits.

Ken Roberts joined us at our table. He has been in real estate development for many years and has had much experience in renovating old buildings, but he never thought about ghosts until coming to Ohio from California and buying the Warehouse on the Canal.

"I've heard footsteps in here when I'm all alone," he said, "as have others. One of the workers who was here alone one night heard footsteps in another room and went out to investigate. He could hear them walking across the wood floors, but there was no one there. He followed the steps out of the room, around a corner into the area where the antique shop is located, where they stopped right up against a wall. Then he heard a door open and close, but he did not see any door. Only later on did we find a door in the wall behind a decorative lattice hung with pictures. That door hasn't been used in years."

"So now you believe in ghosts?" I asked.

"Well, there is certainly something unusual and unexplainable going on here. I've never seen any ghosts here, but others have. A woman was in one of the shops on the second floor around closing time when she saw a man in a tan suit and hat standing there with his back to her. She told the manager that there was still a customer upstairs, but when the manager went up there was no one there. There is only one door for customers to exit downstairs and no man ever came down."

The three of us went down into the basement so Sherri could demonstrate how to use her equipment. The basement was much colder than the upstairs since it was unheated. It wasn't much to look at. Brick walls, concrete floor, one large room with a garage door entrance, a smaller room, and an area with an antiquated freight elevator. Sherri believes the large room was probably where the bodies were prepared for burial. As Ken flicked on the weak lights, she directed her dowsing rods into a particularly dark corner of the room.

"There's usually a lot of energy in this corner," she said, slowly walking toward it, her chrome dowsing rods held out before her. She stopped only a few feet from the wall and, sure enough, the rods began to move, slowly swinging toward each other until they crossed, a positive sign that an energy source had been detected.

Sherri put the rods aside and pointed her EMF meter into the corner. It started crackling, sounding something like static from an old radio, and the red needle swung as far right on the scale as it could go, again indicating a high energy source.

"That's at least a ten on the scale," Sherri said. "Usually, the room reads at about two or three."

Sherri explained that many paranormal investigators believe that ghosts are beings of pure energy, a form of energy common to us all once we die. The idea is based on Einstein's theory that all the energy in the universe is constant. It can neither be created nor destroyed, but it can be transformed into different kinds of energy. So, according to the ghost theory, our living physical energy is transformed into something else when we die: spirit energy. This spirit energy creates electromagnetic disturbances and radical drops in temperature, phenomena that can be measured by scientific equipment.

"But you have to be careful to first rule out any natural expla-nations for the abnormal readings," Sherri said. "If you're standing near the fuse box your EMF readings will be really high, but not because of spirit energy."

Sherri showed me how to use the dowsing rods and I walked around the basement by myself testing them out. It was cold in the basement and the chilly February rain and sleet falling out-side didn't help any, but I didn't feel any sudden temperature drops. I concentrated on the rods in my hands, trying to hold them loose enough to let them move and not so tight that I might subconsciously be moving them myself. Sherri and Ken were working in the other rooms as I walked into the corner Sherri had said contained high energy activity. I stood next to the ramp that was used to roll the gurneys with their shrouded cadavers from the hearse up to the embalming tables. In the gloom, I noticed an old Army-style stretcher leaning against the wall. It was very quiet. I pointed the rods toward the corner and concentrated on what had once taken place in this room. In the shadowed corner, the metal rods caught a glint of light from the single light bulb suspended behind me.

The rod in my right hand began to move.

It was a strange sensation. I could not actually feel the metal rod turning in my hand, but there it was—slowly at first, then a little faster, moving to my left. Then the left-hand rod moved, swinging to the right. As I watched, the rods crossed before me. I was amazed that I had been able to detect an energy source with the rods, despite Sherri's assertion that as much as 80 per-cent of the population could learn to dowse, with a little practice.

From the warehouse, Sherri and I drove to the Pioneer Cemetery, a little plot of land surrounded by a split-rail fence on a side street just across the canal and the Tuscarawas River. The headstones were old—a few from the late eighteenth century—and weathered, some leaning as if about to fall, others snapped in two like broken teeth. We skirted patches of snow and ice as we trudged through the cemetery, dowsing rods in hand. Sherri was going to show me how to "sex a body." I didn't know what she meant, but it sounded good.

She stood in front of and to the side of one of the headstones, about halfway down the gravesite. Using only one rod, she held it out before her over the grave. After a few moments, the rod swung to the left, pointing to the head of the grave. She asked me to read the first name on the stone. I told her it was Elizabeth.

"The rod will point to the head of the deceased if it is a woman, to the feet if it is a man," Sherri said. "I think it's because a woman's energy is concentrated in her head, while a man's energy is concentrated ... lower."

She repeated the test a few more times and was able to accurately determine the gender of the deceased each time.

There was another haunted spot in town that Sherri wanted to show me, again only a short distance from the warehouse: Lock 4 on the Ohio & Erie Canal. A public park now surrounds what is left of the canal and the lock tender's cabin, although on this cold and miserable day there was no one else there.

The lock is part of the 308-mile-long canal that stretched between Cleveland, on Lake Erie, and Portsmouth, on the Ohio River. It was built between 1825–1832. The concrete lock with its wooden gates has been reconstructed and could be operational if the canal were still in use. But the little brick lock tender's cabin is boarded up and crumbling, the solid front door padlocked shut. It seems fitting that the old house remains locked considering what happened there.

By 1857, railroads had already stitched their way across much of America and had rendered the old canal systems obsolete. The Ohio & Erie Canal was no exception and by the mid-1800s was facing financial disaster. It may have been this uncertainty that caused the lock tender to react so violently, or perhaps it was simply part of his rough and alcoholic character to do so—but, in any case, the lock tender grabbed a vat of acid and dumped it over his fellow workers in a fit of rage. Remorse hit him the moment he heard the agonized shrieks of the men and saw their flesh being devoured by the acid. He dumped the rest of the contents of the vat upon himself, adding his dying screams to those of his victims.

The ghost of this tortured man, along with the spirits of those he killed, have been seen drifting among the waterways and by the lock tender's cabin. Some people have taken photographs at night and have found spirit orbs in the developed pictures. We didn't linger in the freezing rain and left Lock 4 to its resident spirits.

Sherri's ghost tour and dinner was the following evening. My wife and I joined approximately forty people at Let's Mango in the Warehouse on the Canal. The group was mixed both by gender and age and included a few people from a ghosthunter's club; half a dozen young men who were just beginning to explore the paranormal world; at least one medium; a "girl's night out" trio of grandmother, daughter, and granddaughter; and the simply curious.

After a presentation by Sherri and a Caribbean-style dinner of roast pork, fried plantains, and potato salad prepared by Margarita Roberts, Sherri led her guests down into the basement where they got to try out the dowsing rods and electronic equipment. People were milling around the dark rooms, lit only by tea lights placed on the floor. Some were working with the dowsing rods. Other people would take pictures of the dowser if the rods crossed; Sherri has a collection of photos showing spirit orbs near the crossed rods of some of her past dowsing guests.

Eva Jean, the elderly woman who identified herself as a medium, felt uncomfortable in the troublesome corner that Sherri had investigated the day before and hung back from it. She did find a spot along the brick wall, however, where she placed her hand and felt a strong psychic energy emanating from it. She was certain that someone had been murdered at that spot, although she could not tell when, nor if the murder actually occurred inside or outside the building.

After the group explored the basement, Sherri and Ken led us all up to the third floor, an open loft with old wooden floors and exposed beams. The freight elevator stopped here, but there was a tall, narrow ladder beside it that led up to the motor maintenance area above the shaft. No one is allowed up there, but some time ago there may have been a little girl who tried to climb up, fell, and was hurt, perhaps killed. I say "perhaps" because the girl is known only through the visions of two people who have sensed her presence. A woman visiting the warehouse had a sudden vision of a little girl lying at the foot of the ladder. It was clear to the woman that the girl was hurt, and the details were so vivid that the visibly distraught woman had to leave the building. Another time, a ten-year-old boy who was using dowsing rods at the foot of the ladder experienced an uncomfortable feeling—"something bad" was how he described it. A photo of him using the rods revealed a brilliant spirit orb floating in the darkness.

As the group investigated the loft I spoke with the medium, Eva Jean. Her silver hair was neatly coiffed and she wore horn-rimmed glasses that didn't quite match her large parrot ear-rings, one teal colored, the other salmon. Eva Jean told me that both her grandfather and father had been spiritualist ministers, so for her, the existence of spirits was not a question. It was an article of faith. She had been in touch with spirits ever since she was a little girl and was quite comfortable with them.

"There's more to fear from the living than there is to fear from the dead," she said.

We hadn't noticed, but as we talked, everyone except Ken and one woman had returned downstairs to the restaurant. The woman stood at the top of the stairs, only a few feet from Eva Jean and me, using dowsing rods. Ken took her picture.

A few days later, Ken e-mailed me the picture. There is Eva Jean and myself talking in the dark loft, there is the woman at the stairs, and there floating among us is a beautiful bright spirit orb.

There is still a lot of research to be done at Warehouse on the Canal. Who or what is causing all the spirit energy that seems to have found a home there? Maybe you will be the one to unlock some of the mysteries.

Central

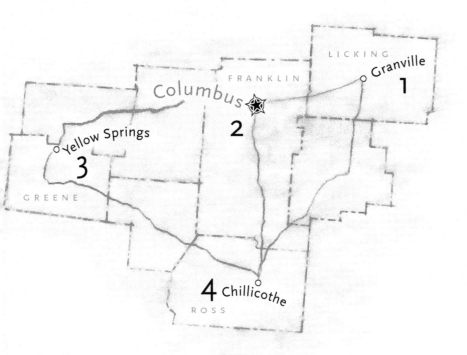

Camp Chase Confederate Cemetery

COLUMBUS

THEY MAY HAVE WORN THE GRAY OR BUTTERNUT UNIFORMS OF THE ARMIES of the Confederate States of America as they fought to secede from the Union, but the memorial that stands in the center of Camp Chase Confederate Cemetery in Columbus reads simply and eloquently, "Americans."

The cemetery is located on Sullivant Avenue in Columbus and is all that remains of the once sprawling Camp Chase, named for Salmon P. Chase, former Ohio governor and Abraham Lincoln's Secretary of the Treasury. During the Civil War, up until November 1861, Camp Chase served as a training camp for Union volunteers. In the early years of the war both sides exchanged prisoners, but that changed once Abraham Lincoln issued his Emancipation Proclamation in 1863. The Confederates were so incensed by Lincoln's audacity—in not only freeing slaves in Southern areas secured by Federal troops, but by putting those same former slaves into Union blue and giving them weapons to fight their former masters—that they declared prisoners would no longer be exchanged. They would be held in detention instead. The Federal government promptly responded in kind. Prisoner of war camps were built on both sides, the most notorious being Andersonville in Georgia.

One of the largest Federal prisoner of war camps was constructed at Camp Chase. At first, Confederates confined there were given a great deal of liberty after swearing an oath of honor. Confederate officers were permitted to wander through Columbus, register in hotels, and receive gifts of money and food. Some even attended sessions of the state senate. The camp became something of a tourist attraction, as paying members of the public were able to visit it. After complaints about the camp's lax discipline and overall poor administration, an investigation was conducted and the situation changed dramatically.

As the war dragged on the camp became overcrowded. Originally designed to house between 3,500 and 4,000 men, by 1863 more than 8,000 prisoners were held at Camp Chase. Two or three men were forced to share each of the single-occupancy bunks, and there were severe shortages of food and medicine as well as clothing and blankets. The barracks were shoddy, the ground was low and usually muddy, and there were open latrines and aboveground open cisterns. As in most Civil War prison camps, even those administered by the most humane officers, disease and malnutrition were widespread under such dire conditions. A smallpox epidemic hit the camp in 1863, decimating the ranks of prisoners. In February of that month alone, 499 men died from smallpox. Between 1861 and 1865 thousands of prisoners died at Camp Chase; 2,260 are buried in the cemetery.

One of them is Benjamin F. Allen of the 50th Tennessee Infantry Regiment, Company D. There is little known about Allen's confinement at Camp Chase or how he died, but he has been the subject of many ghost stories about the Camp Chase Cemetery.

I found his grave on a sunny and unseasonably warm March day with little difficulty. The stone walls of the rectangular cemetery enclose less than two acres and each grave is clearly identified, thanks to the 1906 Act of Congress that provided marble headstones to replace what was left of the old wooden markers. The markers are lined up in military fashion, but there are some gaps where family members have reclaimed the remains of their loved ones and reburied them at home, and there are some sections in which the markers are placed so close together that a person cannot pass between them.

Tombstone said to be visited by the Lady in Gray.

I was the only visitor to the cemetery that day, although I certainly did not feel alone. The cemetery is located on Columbus's west side, and commercial and residential properties butt right up to it on all four sides. In the mid-nineteenth century the cemetery was well outside the city limits, but time and the city's growth have placed the cemetery solidly within the city.

The stone walls muffled the city's sounds, and for a few moments it was possible to concentrate on the men buried beneath the spongy earth and the sacrifices they made for their lost cause. I walked slowly among the graves until I found Allen's.

One story says that there are always fresh flowers placed on Allen's grave, although no one knows who puts them there. No flowers rested upon his grave the day I visited, nor was there any sign that there had been any there recently. In fact, except for one or two miniature Confederate battle flags placed before other headstones, none of the graves had any type of decoration at all.

It is not Benjamin Allen who is said to haunt the Camp Chase Cemetery. Rather, he is the lure for the ghost, a female spirit who has been dubbed the Lady in Gray. Some say that she is the fiancée or wife of Allen and that she continues to mourn the loss of her lover, decorating his grave in his memory.

The Lady in Gray has appeared many times since the cemetery, which fell into disrepair after the war, was renovated and rededicated in 1895 by former Union soldier William H. Knauss. She is a young woman who always appears wearing a gray traveling suit of 1860s vintage trimmed in black. Her hair is pinned up beneath a gray hat and she is always looking down, perhaps weeping. For several years in the late nineteenth century she appeared floating among the trees that dot the cemetery, and hundreds of people swore that they had seen her. In recent years her appearances have been less frequent, but in 1988, during a Civil War re-enactment, several people heard a woman crying. They could find no cause for the sound, nor could they explain the sudden gust of wind that came out of a still and cloudless sky to overturn tents and tables.

There are some who believe the Lady in Gray is the spirit of Louisiana Ransburgh. She was born in Missouri and, when the political feud between pro-Union and pro-Confederate factions in that state erupted in bloodshed, her father sent her away to boarding school at Ohio Wesleyan, just north of Columbus, where he had relatives. The teenaged Louisiana had strong Southern sentiments and had no qualms about voicing them. It has been said that she danced in the streets when Lincoln was assassinated, nearly getting herself lynched in the process.

Ironically, Louisiana fell in love with a Yankee. Joseph Briggs was a wealthy farmer who had also been an Ohio militia captain during the war. They were married in 1867.

By that time Camp Chase had already been closed for two years and most of the buildings had been dismantled. The cemetery was neglected and overgrown with weeds. Many of the wooden grave markers had deteriorated and the original wooden fence that surrounded the grounds was falling apart. Louisiana still harbored sympathies for the dead Confederates, but since she was now married to a respected member of the community—a Northern community—she was more discrete about displaying them. Wearing a heavy veil to conceal her face, Louisiana would venture out at night and slip into the cemetery to lay flowers on the graves.

Could it be the spirit of Louisiana Ransburgh who now haunts the cemetery as the Lady in Gray? Or could there be other women in mourning who drift through the cemetery, looking for their loved ones?

In 1864, six bodies were stolen from the cemetery. Colonel W.P. Richardson of the 25th Ohio Volunteer Infantry reported on November 26, 1864, that, "On the night of the 24th instant the bodies of six deceased prisoners were stole from the grave-yard attached to camp where prisoners only are buried. I arrested the perpetrators of this outrage and referred the matter to General Hooker and was by him directed to turn the prisoners and papers over to the prosecuting attorney of this county, which I have done."

The bodies were never recovered.

Perhaps the Lady in Gray is the beloved of one of these unfortunate men, seeking to be reunited with him in eternity.

The Granville Inn
GRANVILLE

THE VILLAGE OF GRANVILLE HAS BEEN CALLED CEN-
TRAL OHIO'S NEW ENGLAND VILLAGE. Its stately old
homes, tree-lined streets, and old-fashioned shopping district
all look as though they were airlifted right from the Berkshire
Mountains. The New England atmosphere of the village is a
result of the cultural heritage passed on from its original eighteenth-century founders, a company of settlers from Granville,
Massachusetts. They brought with them their Yankee values of
thriftiness and hard work, their love of education, and their
spirituality—and, if The Granville Inn is any indicator, they
may have also brought with them their ghosts.

I first heard about The Granville Inn from a psychic friend of mine, who had gone there for lunch and received strong impressions in the lobby of the inn. She was unable to be more explicit than that, but she did suggest that the inn was worth investigating.

The inn's owner and general manager, Tony Beckerley, was cordial when I spoke to him on the phone and told him that I would like to ghosthunt the inn. He told me that he had never experienced any paranormal events there, but that I was welcomed to speak with his staff about any experiences they might have had.

Mary and I arrived at The Granville Inn on a rainy Sunday in March. Even under gray skies, the inn was impressive. It sat well back from the street, beyond an expansive lawn and ancient trees. Ivy crept up the native sandstone walls of the building, and large, leaded-glass windows looked out onto the gardens at the front of the inn. A large flagstone terrace extended from the front of the inn, unused now in the chill of March; in warmer months an awning would extend over outdoor diners. The inn looked every inch like an English country manor.

There was a cheery fire glowing in the fireplace in the lobby, a nice touch considering the chilly rain outside. Two wing chairs sat by the large leaded glass windows. Oriental rugs covered the wood floors, which matched the paneled oak walls. We arrived as Sunday brunch was being served in the main dining room behind the lobby.

We were shown to our room, one of the twenty-seven rooms and three suites that comprise the inn. It was small but comfortable, furnished in English country style with casement windows that gave us a view of the front lawn and an occasional car passing by on East Broadway.

Tony had told me that the night desk manager may have some stories for me when he came on duty, so I had plenty of time to explore the inn on my own before then. Although the dining room downstairs was busy, the rest of the inn was quiet; there would be few guests that night besides Mary and me. I wandered around on the second floor, but there was little to see except numbered guest room doors and linen closets. One door, however, was marked Club Room, and when I opened it I found a set of carved, wooden stairs that led up to a large carpeted common room. There was a sofa facing a television, comfortable chairs, card tables, and an old-fashioned pool table. A large pendulum clock hung on the wall, softly ticking off the seconds with every stroke. The room was empty.

A short hall to one side of the room led to one of the suites. At the other end of the common room was an emergency fire door, behind which I found out later was an unfinished room used for storage. It was from that attic room's window that employees leaving the inn for the night would see a light shining, even though they knew no one was up there and the light had been off.

That night I met with Ralph. It was about 11 P.M. when I left my room and went downstairs to talk with him. The inn was silent as I came down the stairs and passed beneath the chandeliers in the lobby. The entire first floor was paneled floor-to-ceiling in dark oak. The chandeliers reflected off the gleaming oak, but even so, the dark wood and thick silence made me feel like I was creeping through the Wuthering Heights estate. I walked down the wide hall, past the now-dark main dining room, to the lounge in the rear where Ralph sat alone, smoking a cigarette. Ralph was watching some cop show on the television mounted above the bar. He used the remote to turn down the volume a little as I pulled out a chair and sat at the table with him, but he didn't turn it off. Behind him, the walls were lined with windows, black now as the rainy night slammed up against them.

Ralph told me he had worked at the inn for twenty-six years, beginning as a waiter. In all that time he had never seen a ghost there, although he and a couple of other waiters did carry out from the dining room, chair and all, a ninety-six-year-old woman who had died at dinner.

"We tried to be discrete about it," Ralph said, blowing a stream of cigarette smoke skyward.

Ralph did experience something unusual at the inn, however. All right, *more* unusual. It had happened several years ago and only once, but Ralph remembers vividly the night he walked into the cold spot.

"It happened right out there," he said, gesturing to the hall outside the lounge. "I was at the front desk and I was coming down the hall to sweep it, when I walked into this icy cold wall. There's no other way to describe it. The hair on my arms and the back of my neck lifted up—I could feel it, and I was suddenly sick to my stomach."

Ralph couldn't bring himself to push past the wall, so he returned to the desk.

"Half an hour or so later, I tried again and this time there was no problem. Whatever had been there was gone."

Ralph had no idea what caused the cold wall, but he said that Ed, a previous night manager, had encountered exactly the same phenomenon and had refused to go back down the hall.

I walked with Ralph back to the front desk. He paused in the hall to show me the spot at which he had run into the psychic wall.

"Right here," he said, spreading his arms, and I could see by the look upon his face that he was still confused by whatever it was he had run into that night.

Cold spots and lights in the attic. Small beginnings for a ghost story, but the following morning yielded even stranger experiences from some of the inn's employees.

Susie Robertson has been the Granville Inn's bookkeeper for three years. Her windowless office is tucked away in a corner of the basement, a place where she hears all the creaks, groans, and rattles of the old inn, built in 1924. "I know all those noises well and am not bothered by them, but the tapping I heard that particular night was something new," she said.

Susie said that, as she was working alone in her office one night, she heard an odd tapping sound coming from the room next door. Curious, since the only other person in the entire building was the desk clerk on the first floor, she decided to investigate. She followed the sound to the room next door, but when she went inside it abruptly stopped. Then she heard it behind her, in a different room. She followed the sound to that room and again, when she entered, it stopped, only to start up in yet another location. This continued for a while, the weird tapping leading her on a merry chase through the various rooms in the basement and up the backstairs into the kitchen. Nothing in the hall. Nothing in the kitchen storeroom. She walked into the empty kitchen. Nothing. She jumped when a pan suddenly fell off a shelf and clattered to the floor. Susie told the manager what had happened, but no one was ever able to explain the tapping sounds she heard that night.

In addition to the tapping, Susie has also felt strange chills in the basement and the sensation that there was some presence nearby, even though nothing was ever seen.

"I've had those same feelings as well," said Kim Palmer, the inn's office manager. "I've felt a presence, a pressure so strong that I felt I couldn't breathe."

Kim also told me about the woman who called down to the switchboard in the middle of the night, demanding a room change. "The woman said that her little boy was terrified by something in the room, although she refused to say exactly what it was, and wanted me to move her family immediately to a different room, which I did. It was very weird."

One of the strangest things to happen at the Granville Inn occurred to Diane Kelley, the inn's catering and events director. During a severe summer storm in 2003, the inn lost all its electrical power. The kitchen could not function so the inn was

closed for lunch and dinner. Diane said that it was very peaceful at the inn that afternoon, since there were no visitors and
the loss of power made it unusually quiet. She curled up in one
of the wing chairs in the lobby and enjoyed the unusual respite
from her normal duties.

She was alone in the lobby. After a few minutes of watching
the storm outside, Diane turned and saw that the chandelier at
the foot of the stairs across the lobby was swinging.

"It wasn't a gentle motion," she said. "It was swinging wildly
back and forth as if it were on a ship. It was like someone
whacked it with something." Diane and I were standing at the
foot of the stairs, below the chandelier, a brass hexagonal
lantern. There were two other lights nearby, but Diane said
that neither of them had stirred at all.

"I couldn't believe what I was seeing," she said. "I got up and
walked over to it and stood there looking at it. Then, one of the
glass panes lifted out of the lantern and *floated* down to the floor.
I screamed and the manager came running out of his office. I
told him what happened. He picked up the glass and brought it
back to his office. The whole thing gives me goose bumps just
talking about it," Diane said, and a noticeable tremor passed
through her body.

I reached up and touched the lantern, pushing it gently and
letting it swing. It was lighter than it looked but still heavy
enough to require one serious wind to move it. I looked around
for some obvious explanation for the swinging light but could
find nothing. The only nearby window is in the stairwell, but
the inn is air-conditioned and the window is never opened, so
there is no chance it could have admitted a gust of wind to set
the chandelier in motion. There was nothing in the area that
could have somehow knocked against the light.

Diane has also felt a strange sensation pass across the backs
of her legs and neck when she goes up the stairs to the Club

Room. She feels uncomfortable on those stairs, although she can't explain why. She hopes to hold a séance in the Club Room with some of the other employees to see if they can find out who or what haunts the inn.

No one knows yet what is going on there, but a careful examination of the history of the site may eventually provide some answer to the mystery. What is known is that the site upon which The Granville Inn stands today was the site of the very first frame house erected in Granville, built by Timothy Spelman in 1805. In later years another owner added a tavern and, still later, the building became a bank. In 1838, a four-story frame structure was built to house the Granville Female College, which tutored young ladies for sixty years before closing its doors in 1898. The building then served briefly as a Methodist home for the aged until it was torn down in 1908. The Granville Inn was constructed on the site in 1934.

With such a diverse and colorful history, with so many people coming and going on the site, there is, no doubt, enough psychic energy there for at least one ghost, if not several. Perhaps in time we will know them by name.

The Lofts Hotel
COLUMBUS

SHE IS WHAT SOME PSYCHIC INVESTIGATORS CALL
A "CORNER GHOST," a spirit seen only with one's peripheral vision that disappears when looked at directly. Even so, the
Lady of The Lofts Hotel is a very active spirit, having appeared
frequently to several staff members of this elegant boutique
hotel in downtown Columbus's new Arena District.

The Lady, often described as attired in Victorian clothing, is
simultaneously at home and lost in the five-story brick Carr
Building, erected in 1882, which now houses The Lofts Hotel
and its forty-four New York loft-style rooms. From 1882 to 1932
the Columbus Transfer Company worked out of the building,

followed in 1936 by the Carr Plumbing Supply Company, and then by an architectural firm until The Lofts opened its doors in 1998. The Lady no doubt still recognizes the floor-to-ceiling windows, wood floors, brick walls, and exposed beams, but must be confused by the sleek chrome and cherry wood furniture, the mini-bar, cable TV, and Internet access in every room. Perhaps that is why she mostly confines herself to the stairwell off the lobby, especially the area between the first and second floors.

"The first time I saw her was in 1999," said Dawn Minnick, one of the hotel's concierges, "but I've seen her often since then, maybe once or twice a month. She's always been between the first and second floors, about to turn the stairs. If I turn to look at her head-on she vanishes."

Dawn talked about the Lady as being a corner ghost, and her description of the spirit's manifestations fit the definition. Some researchers believe that ghosts are visible only in the infrared zone, which would render them invisible to humans, since we cannot see into the infrared zone naturally. Humans are not entirely infrared blind, however. There is a thin band around the outer edge of the cornea that is sensitive to some degree of infrared light. That outer ring constitutes our peripheral vision, so if ghosts inhabit the infrared range, it would make sense that they would best be seen peripherally, that is, from the "corner of our eye." This theory may also explain why digital cameras seem so adept at capturing spirits, since digital cameras can "see" into the infrared zone.

It was late on a Friday night and Dawn was seated at her desk in the little lobby as we talked. She was in uniform, wearing the gray blazer, black pants, and black-and-gold scarf of the concierge. She was excited by her encounters with the paranormal and spoke about them at length, now and then interrupted by people coming and going from Max & Erma's Restaurant, which adjoins the hotel.

"The first time I saw her I was stunned and felt scared. I looked like I had seen a ghost," Dawn said, aware of the irony. "I've seen her so often since that first time, though, that I know now there is no reason to be afraid of her."

That first encounter with the Lady of The Lofts occurred shortly after Dawn had begun working at the hotel. She was walking up the stairs from the basement to the first floor landing when suddenly, in her peripheral vision, she saw a shadowy figure descending the stairs from the landing, heading right for her. Startled, Dawn turned to get a better look and the figure disappeared. In those few seconds Dawn was able to see a long dark skirt and white blouse, clothes that she described as having a "Victorian feel" to them. Each time that Dawn has seen the Lady since then, it has always been under similar circumstances and the clothes have remained the same. It's almost as if psychic videotape is playing on a continuous loop in that stairwell.

After Dawn and I spoke a little longer I decided to check out the stairwell for myself. The first thing I noticed when I opened the door and stepped inside was that the stairwell had, like the rest of the building, been renovated. Bright, modern lighting flooded the stairs, even at that late hour of the night, so there were no natural shadows or gloomy corners that could easily be mistaken for some otherworldly spirit. The second thing I noticed was how loud it was in the stairwell. The stairs were made of iron and clanged loudly with every step I took; a mouse would have sounded like an elephant on those stairs. This is important since Dawn said that the Lady was completely silent as she descended the stairs, an impossibility for any flesh-and-blood creature.

I walked up and down the stairs a few times, taking pictures as I went, before finally turning in for the night in my fourth-floor room. Worn out from hiking the stairs, I slept like a dead man.

The next morning I met with the hotel's general manager, Kathyrn Cobern. Her office was located in the basement, and I walked down, rather than riding the elevator, in the hope of catching a glimpse of the Lady. No luck. Kathyrn's office was furnished in the same spare modern style as the guest rooms, but her friendly and energetic demeanor made it seem warmer.

When she came to The Lofts Hotel in 2003 the other employees immediately apprised Kathryn of the existence of the ghost, but she thought they were all teasing her, maybe just having a little fun with the new girl. Even so, she decided to speak to the ghost whenever she was on the stairs, just in case.

"I would introduce myself out loud," she said, "telling her I was the new general manager and that I would like to meet her. And then I did."

One night, shortly after she had started working at the hotel, Kathyrn was in the stairwell between the first and second floors when she saw the same "corner ghost" that Dawn had seen. Kathyrn's description of the ghost was essentially the same as Dawn's, though a little more detailed. Kathyrn described a long dark skirt and white blouse with a lacy collar, and said the ghost wore her hair up in a bun.

Large archival photos from Columbus's past hang on the walls of the hotel, both in the public areas and in the guest rooms. In one of those old black-and-white photos—a group of men and women gathered in front of a grocery store—Kathryn spotted the ghost. The woman is wearing Victorian-style clothing with a long dark skirt and her hair is pulled up into a bun. She holds a baby wrapped in a white blanket in her arms. Even though no one in the hotel has seen or heard the baby, Kathryn has a strong feeling that the woman in the photo is the Lady of The Lofts.

No one knows the identity of the woman in the photo or her connection to the Carr Building, which is now the hotel. Kathryn does have a theory about the ghost's identity, however.

"We haven't been able to prove it," she said, "but there is a story that a woman once died in an elevator accident in this building many years ago. That could explain why the ghost is always on the stairs."

"She's afraid of dying again?" I asked, aware of the irony yet again.

Kathyrn nodded her head. "Could be. You know, I was a total skeptic before I saw her."

"And now you believe in ghosts?"

"There is definitely a spirit here," she said. "I've seen it more than once."

Kathyrn had just seen the Lady only a week before my stay at the hotel. She told me that she was about to go downstairs to her office, following just behind a hotel guest who was a hockey player. He held the door open for her but then her cell phone rang. She stopped to answer it and motioned for the guest to go on. She heard him clomping up the steps. She started down the stairs a few moments later and there she was, the Lady of The Lofts, silently drifting toward her. Once again, in the brief time Kathyrn saw the ghost, she recognized its now trademark clothing and hairstyle.

Zach Cook, a young marketing major at Ohio State University, earns money to help pay his tuition bills by working as a parking valet at The Lofts. He saw the ghost only two months after being hired. He was sheepish in talking about the ghost as we sat in the lobby because he had never believed in ghosts before. Now he wasn't so sure. He said he was coming up the stairs from the basement when he spotted the ghost coming down the stairs ahead of him. Before she vanished, he said, he noticed that she wore a costume that looked like "an old white wedding gown."

Jessica Moody is yet another employee of The Lofts who has had a run-in with the ghost. Jessica has worked as a concierge at the hotel for almost three years, but didn't have her first encounter with the ghost until only four months before I met her.

"I had heard all the stories about her," Jessica said, "and finally, after two and a half years, I saw her. It freaked me out." Jessica also described the ghost's hair as "pulled up in a bun" and said she wore a long hoop skirt. "I saw her on the first floor landing just floating, coming down the stairs. It was the first time I had ever seen a ghost," she said. "I was a skeptic, but no more."

Jessica added two new elements to The Lofts ghost story that I had not yet heard. She said that the elevators have been seen to come and go on their own, the doors opening and closing without anyone there, at least, no one visible. Further, she said that a female guest on the fifth floor had seen a hazy figure, a woman in a hoop skirt, in the hallway.

It seemed like the Lady of The Lofts was finding her way out of the stairwell after all.

Kathyrn Cobern might agree. On more than one occasion, she has felt a strong presence in the hall outside her basement office at night. Not a malevolent feeling, but one that makes your skin tingle—the gut feeling that you are not alone, even though your five senses insist that you are.

Sensing the presence of a ghost is one thing, but being touched by one is quite another. Diane Brown has been a housekeeper at the hotel since 1998, and in all that time has never seen the ghost. She's heard all the stories, of course, and has heard footsteps and doors opening and closing, but those events could probably be explained by the public nature of the hotel. People come and go all the time. Still, Diane knows what she felt.

We were talking in the hall on the fourth floor where she had parked her housekeeping cart. She told me about the day a few years ago when she had been working on the second floor. She had stooped to pick up a room service tray from the floor and, as she stood up, someone or something rapped her across the back of her head.

"It was hard, too," Diane said. "I stood up, rubbing my head, trying to figure out what had hit me. A guest came out of his room just then and saw me looking around, rubbing my head. He must have thought I was crazy."

Diane checked the cart to see if there was anything that projected from it or that could have fallen off to hit her. Nothing. Nor was there anything projecting from the walls. In fact, nothing anywhere near her could have struck her.

"I've never been able to explain it," she said.

I spent two nights at The Lofts, a good deal of that time in the stairwell—maybe people thought I was crazy—but the Lady chose not to reveal herself to me. No surprise, really. Ghost-hunting requires an inordinate amount of patience; ghosts do not respond well to command performances.

I remember Dawn Minnick telling me that the Lady does not appear to guests—the woman who Jessica mentioned being the single exception to date—but seems to restrict her visits to employees. Still, if the Lady of The Lofts Hotel has made an exception once, then she can again. Maybe you'll be the next guest to see her.

Majestic Theatre

CHILLICOTHE

**THERE IS A CRIMSON SMEAR ACROSS THE BLACK,
VARNISHED FLOORBOARDS** of the stage at the Majestic
Theatre, a reflection from the exit sign in the wings at stage left.
It looks like blood.

And why not blood?

When the Spanish influenza ripped through the troops who
were waiting to ship out to Europe from nearby Camp Sherman
to fight the Germans in 1918, so many soldiers died that the
local Chillicothe mortuaries were overwhelmed and quickly ran
out of space. A now-defunct mortuary that was located across
the street from the Majestic used the theater as an additional

morgue for the more than 1,200 fatalities from the Army training camp. A contemporary observer noted that the soldiers'
bodies were "stacked like cordwood" in the dressing rooms below
the stage until they could be brought up on stage to be embalmed
beneath the bright theater lights. In the rush to embalm so many
bodies quickly, certain niceties were overlooked; the blood and
bodily fluids of the poor victims were pumped out into the alley
behind the theater, earning it the nickname it holds to this day,
"Blood Alley."

So maybe the scarlet streak on the floor was a reflection, but
did not the blood of so many dead men leave an indelible stain
upon the floorboards of the Majestic Theatre? Are their spirits
not forever linked to that place?

There are many who believe they are.

"I have worked here for ten years and have never experienced
anything out of the ordinary," said Marti Oyer, manager of the
theater. I found her at her desk in the second-floor box office,
surrounded by old photos and movie posters.

Marti may have not seen any ghosts, but the sweatshirt she
was wearing—a colorful cartoon print of Scooby-Doo being
chased by ghosts beneath a Frankenstein-green "Boo!" logo—
simply begged me to ask her about them.

"I just tell them that if they don't bother me I won't bother
them," she explained. "But there are so many different stories
people tell about this place."

The Majestic Theatre has been around long enough to earn
its reputation for being haunted. It is the oldest freestanding
theater in America. Originally built as the Masonic Opera
House in 1852, the theater is something of a shrine to the history of entertainment in this country. It first hosted the dramas,
minstrel shows, comedies, and farces popular in the mid-nineteenth century, then later vaudeville and burlesque shows, and
finally, films. Today, the theater, which is run by a non-profit

organization dedicated to preserving the Majestic, features both films and live theatrical performances.

Marti filled me in on some of the stories about the Majestic before pausing in her conversation to take care of a customer who had come in to purchase tickets for an upcoming perform-ance. I stepped out of the office and examined a tall glass case filled with Majestic Theatre memorabilia. The faded photos and yellowing programs and posters displayed in the case portrayed a proud theatrical history one would never have thought possi-ble in this little heartland theater. Buffalo Bill Cody, Ole Bull, Laurel and Hardy, Lynn Fontaine, Eddie Foy, George M. Cohan, Sophie Tucker, Milton Berle, Bob Hope—each of them had trod the boards at the Majestic.

While Marti waited on her customer, I walked up the few steps to the door to the balcony. I opened it and walked in. It was dark and it took my eyes a few moments to adjust to the gloom. I was standing in the rear of the balcony, looking down at the stage. Even in the low light, the theater was beautiful. Below me the stage was lit by only a row of footlights. The wall was scarlet and the stage itself was picture-framed in a blue border trimmed with gilded accents, a wreath, and musical instruments. Two large carved and gilded medallions anchored the top corners of the frame. The red curtain hanging above the stage was embroi-dered with an ornate "M," surrounded by a wreath.

Frescos along the sides of the theater depicted the four seasons. There were blank white panels on the walls around the balcony. At one time they had contained frescos that were considered too vulgar by the women of the town and, so, were painted over.

As I stood at the rear of the balcony, the polished brass rail before me glowing faintly in the dim light, it was easy to imag-ine what it would have been like in the old days of the theater, to be sitting there in the dark, losing yourself in whatever fan-tasy was being played out on stage. I could see Laurel and

Hardy or Milton Berle on stage and could almost hear the audience laughing.

I remembered then that ghostly laughter had been recorded on tape in the theater. A group of students from the University of Akron who were studying paranormal activity had visited the theater in 2001. They set up cameras and tape recorders in two locations in the theater and left them on overnight. When they played back the tape recorder the next day they heard a little girl singing and asking, "How do I get out of here?"

The same child's voice had also been heard during a 1994 taping of the TV show *Cash Explosion* at the theater. After the director had called for quiet on the set, he heard the ghostly singing in his headset. There was no child in the theater.

Marti told me that many years ago a little girl had been murdered and her body dumped in the theater. Could it be this little girl, dubbed "Elizabeth" by theater volunteers, whose shadowy form has been seen running in the dressing rooms and stage area? Is it her image actors have seen appear for only an instant in their dressing room mirrors?

Little Elizabeth, however, is not a solo act at the Majestic. She has ghostly co-stars as well.

One of them was seen in 2000 when the theater's technical director, with the aid of two high school boys, was replacing the huge white curtain that surrounds the stage. They had just finished their work and had left the stage when one of the boys noticed someone standing onstage. He told the director that someone was there. The director knew that the theater was empty except for the three of them, but he thought that perhaps he had left some lights on that were making shadows. He went back onto the stage to check the lights. The boy called to him that the person was behind the curtain. As the director crossed the stage the boy yelled that the thing was also walking, heading right for him. The director said he didn't see anything, but suddenly felt enveloped in a freezer-cold spot. The three of them made a hasty exit out of the theater.

Could the thing onstage have been the spirit of one of the poor soldiers from Camp Sherman? And is this apparition responsible for the mysterious cloud that formed on the stage and rose high above it into the catwalk, terrorizing a workman who nearly fell off the catwalk as he tried to escape from the strange fog?

I left the balcony and walked down the dark main aisle of the theater to the stairs leading to the dressing rooms below the stage. The maroon and yellow palm-frond carpeting in the theater gave way to bare concrete as I descended below stage. I was in a narrow, low-ceilinged hall. The walls were made of white-washed brick. Pipes snaked above me. Somewhere I heard water dripping. Cramped little dressing rooms opened up off the corridor. I was reminded of the catacombs in Rome. The dressing rooms were Spartan, to say the least. The same white bricks, perhaps a metal chair or two, a mirror. Each door was marked with a wooden star, the original bronze stars having been stolen long ago. The dressing rooms were not designed for comfort or idle lounging, and considering their grisly history—the pale, stiff corpses of young soldiers piled high within them—who would want to linger there?

Not me.

I came up from the dressing area and walked back up to Marti's office. She was talking to someone on the telephone. She hung up and turned to me in her swivel chair.

"How did it go?" she asked.

"Great," I said. "I took some pictures."

"Those students from Akron I told you about, they took pictures, too. Upstairs in the Knights' Room."

"Can you show me the room?"

Marti led me out of the office and across the lobby behind the balcony. We entered a wide staircase that had clearly been designed as a grand entrance to the Masonic lodge rooms above. Unlike the rest of the theater, the staircase and the upper floor had not yet been renovated. The stairs were wide and solid, turning once as they ascended, the whole affair enclosed by a sturdy wooden balustrade. The walls, now stripped of any ornamentation, were flaking gray paint. A large window at the top of the stairs flooded light into the stairwell. The steps creaked beneath our feet as we climbed to the top.

The upper floor, added by the Masons in 1876, was nothing like the theater below. The two main rooms were the ballroom and the Knights' Room, both of which had ceilings that were at least twelve feet high. Wallpaper that had once covered the walls had been pulled down, revealing frescos painted back in the late 1800s when the Masons had used these rooms for their secret ceremonies.

We stepped into the Knights' Room.

"The people from Akron set up a video camera in here," Marti said. "When they played back the tape, they saw orbs in the room. Orbs are supposed to be ghosts. They set up the camera a second time and got the same results."

Several large windows along one side of the room filled the space with light. Outside I could see the rooftops of Chillicothe and, in the distance, the same blue hills that appear on the official seal of the State of Ohio. Nothing very ghostly about the setting, I thought. Still, I took a few photos in the room.

I didn't want to impose on Marti's time much more, so I asked her if I could look around for a while on my own, allowing her to return to her work. After Marti had left I stood in the Knights' Room for several minutes, quietly, unmoving, simply letting the aura of the room wash over me.

There were several near life-sized frescos of knights painted on the walls. Each of them stood in a three-dimensional painted niche. They wore long white cloaks over white tunics, the red cross of the Knights Templar—a society every bit as secretive as the Masons—prominent on their left shoulders. The frescos were faded and peeling in spots, but were not beyond restoration.

The ceiling was another matter. Marked with water stains and pocked with holes, ragged curls of wallpaper and broken pieces of plaster dangled from it. In places the lathing showed through and specks of daylight were visible.

Fresco of a Knight Templar in the Majestic Theatre's Knights' Room.

The room's overall effect was like stepping into a medieval hall that had been neglected over the centuries by an aristocratic family now down on its luck. Nothing a lot of money and a lot of labor couldn't fix.

I stood in the silent room, the eyes of the knights upon me, and felt a sense of tranquility and peace, something like meditating in a twelfth-century chapel in Tuscany. There was a small room off the Knights' Room, and I walked over to investigate. As I stood in the doorway looking into the room, which held nothing but a jumble of old plumbing fixtures, my back to the Knights' Room,

I felt the undeniable presence of someone behind me. I wanted to turn around but didn't, instead letting the feeling build up within me. I was not afraid, but felt an intense curiosity. My ears strained to pick up any sound behind me, but there was nothing. Still, the feeling that something or someone stood behind me was overwhelming. At last I turned, slowly, hoping that whatever was there would still be there when I turned around. There was nothing. That evening, when I downloaded my photos into my computer, a single orb showed up, floating in the Knights' Room.

The adjacent ballroom was a much larger room than the Knights' Room. It, too, had frescos decorating the walls. A huge landscape fresco in very bad condition dominated one wall. Some old theater seats were stacked in the room, as were assorted pieces of dusty theater equipment no longer in use. Here, too, the ceiling was a disaster waiting to happen.

At one time, this floor was connected to a hotel, which has since been torn down. The Masons and their guests would often stay in the hotel, and over the years it, too, developed a reputation as a haunted place. One wonders if perhaps those hotel ghosts, having been permanently checked out, have taken up residence in the Majestic Theatre instead. What else would explain the many orbs photographed in those rooms?

The Majestic Theatre has enjoyed a long and interesting history as a center for quality entertainment. The tradition continues today, and it's worth taking in a show there. You never know who or what you will see.

Ye Olde Trail Tavern

YELLOW SPRINGS

THE SLEEPY LITTLE VILLAGE OF YELLOW SPRINGS was originally known for the medicinal sulphur springs that gave the community its name. Later, it became known as the home of Antioch College, one of the most liberal and challenging colleges in the country (and also my alma mater). Ye Olde Trail Tavern has been a silent witness to much of the village's history, beginning with the travelers who rested at this stagecoach stop in the early nineteenth century, and continuing to the present generation of Antioch students who stop in to slake their thirst.

Another silent witness to Yellow Springs's history is the Blue Lady, the ghost of Ye Olde Trail Tavern.

"I'm very careful what I say about her," said Cathy Christian, who has owned the tavern for eighteen years now. "She's been quiet recently and I don't want to stir things up."

We were talking at the bar in the front of the tavern. Cathy is a middle-aged woman with a pleasant disposition and had no qualms about telling me her ghost stories, although she also cautioned me that she never makes fun of the ghost and that I shouldn't either. She learned her lesson the hard way, she said. One day two of her friends who had heard stories about the Blue Lady visited the tavern. Cathy hid herself in the women's restroom, standing on the toilet so that her feet wouldn't show. She jumped out at them with a resounding *"Boo!"* and scared the wits out of her friends. One of them ran screaming all the way back downstairs.

"I thought it was a great joke," Cathy said, "until I came into work the next day and found that all my refrigerator cases had frozen up. All the produce, the milk, everything was frozen solid. I called in a repairman and he could not find any reason why that would have happened. The refrigerators were working fine. I had to pitch all that food. It cost me a lot of money, so I'm careful what I say about her these days."

"Alright, I'll try not to make any jokes," I said.

"One of my regulars was right here at the bar talking about her and he said he didn't believe in her, in ghosts at all. The moment he said that, the glass ashtray before him snapped in two."

Before I could help myself I asked, "Was he in her no smoking section?"

Cathy gave me a warning look and I thought maybe I should take her advice and be quiet for a while. "Do you mind if I look around?" I asked.

"Help yourself," she said.

The tavern was built in 1827 by Francis Hafner to serve travelers along the Cincinnati-Columbus stagecoach route. The first floor is dark, a result of the low-ceilinged architectural style of the nineteenth century. I walked past the bar into the main dining room, the old wood floor creaking beneath my feet. This was the original structure built by Hafner. It was a dark room furnished with dark wood furniture, long pioneer-style tables with benches, and high-backed booths. Exposed beams crossed the low ceiling, and antique tools, hardware, and farm implements hung from them. A rough stone fireplace stood at the far end of the room. Old cooking pots and skillets hung from the mantel. I could see how a ghost would fit right in with the décor. In the gloom of that room I could almost see Daniel Boone and Simon Kenton huddled near the fire sipping from tankards of ale.

But the ghost is that of a woman.

Jake* has worked at Ye Olde Trail Tavern for sixteen years. He came into the dining room and I asked him what he knew about the ghost. He said he had never seen it nor had he had any interaction with it, but he said that several people had seen her over the years. Jake was tall with short hair and an earring in his right ear. He had the friendly personality necessary for success in the restaurant business, but he talked about the ghost in an offhand manner, as if perhaps he wasn't a believer.

"They always describe a lady in a blue dress," he said, "an old-fashioned style. She has her hair pulled up in a bun."

"What's her story?" I asked.

"No one knows, really," Jake said. "I had heard something about her husband going off to war and never returning and so she's waiting for him to come back. People see her upstairs mostly."

After we talked, I took down the "Employees Only" chain and went up the narrow stairs to the second floor. It was just as dark here as it was downstairs, maybe darker. I stood on the tiny landing at the top of the stairs. To my right was a storage room. The door was opened. Wood floors and exposed beams as below. Tall shelves crammed with canned goods, gallon-sized jars of condiments, and other packaged foods stood beneath the sloping attic roof. On the opposite wall another set of shelves held additional dinnerware and crockery.

To my left, off a narrow hall no more than six feet long, was the former women's restroom and Cathy's office. Years ago the office had been a private dining room, but it was so far removed from the rest of the tavern that it became inconvenient for use in that manner.

I stood in the dim hallway, listening. There was no one else upstairs, and the downstairs dining room was quiet since I was visiting the tavern before its regular business hours. Cathy had said that the ghost had not been active for a while, and I didn't get a sense of her that day. I went back downstairs.

I rejoined Cathy where she was stocking the bar and told her I had been upstairs, and also told her how Jake had described the ghost.

"Everyone sees a lady in blue," she said, "but some see her with her hair up, others have seen her with long hair hanging down. I don't know, can a ghost change her hairstyle?"

That sounded like a joke to me and I was going to warn her, but I figured she knew her resident ghost a lot better than I did.

"It seems like guys with ponytails are the people who see her," she said.

My immediate thought was that in a liberal college town like Yellow Springs, there should be no shortage of pony-tailed male witnesses, but I didn't say that. "Do you suppose it's because they remind her of someone with their old hairstyle?"

"Could be, I don't know."

She told me that both a cook and a manager at the tavern had seen the ghost.

The manager was alone at night, after closing. He had sent everyone home, locked the door, and was counting the day's receipts. He heard a noise, looked up, and saw a woman in a blue and white dress coming in the front door. The dress had a high collar. She was in her thirties, with light-colored hair pulled up in a bun. The manager told her the tavern was closed, but the mysterious woman did not answer. She only smiled and walked closer to the bar where he was working. He told her once more that she would have to leave since the tavern was closed, but she ignored him and walked on into the dining room. The manager went after her, but when he got to the dining room the woman was gone. He looked all over the building, but she was nowhere to be found.

The cook's brush with the ghost occurred on the second floor, just outside the ladies' room. There, standing in the darkness, he saw a woman with long black hair, wearing an ankle-length dark dress. Her face was hidden in shadow, but even without seeing her expression, the cook got the impression that she was sad. He also thought the ghost was one of his co-workers until he went downstairs and asked another worker what was wrong with Elaine*. The other answered that he did not know, since Elaine was on vacation in Michigan and not at the restaurant. When the cook went back upstairs, the woman had vanished.

"So, who do you think the woman is?" I asked.

Cathy didn't know.

At one point in its history the building housed a bakery. There is a story that the wife of the baker was having an affair with the village postmaster, whose office was right across the street. It is said that one of the men—which one is lost to history—was found dead in the street with an ice pick in his eye. If the story is true, which man does the ghost mourn? Her lover? Her husband? Both?

The identity of the Blue Lady might never be discovered, but if anyone can discover it, Lemoine Rice is the man. Rice is a paranormal investigator who has held several ghost classes at the tavern.

"He scares me more than the ghost," Cathy said, referring to Rice's ability to communicate with the Blue Lady. "One time he told me that she wanted us to put up a Christmas tree. He also knew how afraid I was of the ghost and encouraged me to talk with her, to sort of make my peace with her.

"I used to come into work at eight in the morning, but that is when things would happen. I was alone and it scared me. One day I came in and, as I was working here at the bar, the light cords from the wall lamps pulled out of their sockets and started whipping hard against the wall."

I looked at one of the lights, a lantern-style fixture mounted on the wall. A short cord ran from the light to the outlet below it. There was no way that cord could have simply dropped out of the outlet and begin beating itself against the wall.

"After the lights incident, I thought maybe I would do what Lemoine suggested," Cathy said. "So one morning, when I was all alone, I started talking to the ghost, just asking it to stop scaring me and leave me in peace.

"I didn't tell anyone about it, but the next time I saw Lemoine he said he knew I had talked to the ghost. That wasn't the half of it. He repeated to me, almost word for word, what I had said. He said the ghost told him that."

If Rice can contact the ghost, maybe someone will eventually be able to capture her image on film. So far, all attempts to do so have failed. A reporter once came to the tavern to write about the ghost. She was particularly interested in photographing the portraits hanging in Cathy's office, but she could not get her camera to work properly when she was up there. She took the camera downstairs, where it worked without problem. She went back upstairs to the office and once again the camera failed. The reporter could find no explanation for why it would not work in the office. I had no difficulty with my camera when I was there, but the pictures did not reveal anything unusual.

No one knows whether or not the Blue Lady still haunts Ye Olde Trail Tavern. Cathy said that things have been quiet for a while, perhaps as a result of her little tête-à-tête with the ghost, but she doesn't take that as a guarantee that all is well. Who knows? Cathy may be more attuned to the ways of the spirit world than the rest of us. She may know that ghosts are restless spirits, and that one can never be sure if they have departed or linger still for one last nightcap.

Southwest

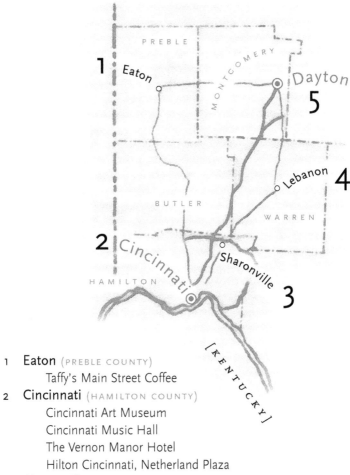

1 **Eaton** (PREBLE COUNTY)
  Taffy's Main Street Coffee
2 **Cincinnati** (HAMILTON COUNTY)
  Cincinnati Art Museum
  Cincinnati Music Hall
  The Vernon Manor Hotel
  Hilton Cincinnati, Netherland Plaza
3 **Sharonville** (HAMILTON COUNTY)
  Heritage Village Museum
4 **Lebanon** (WARREN COUNTY)
  The Golden Lamb Inn
5 **Dayton** (MONTGOMERY COUNTY)
  US Air Force Museum
  Woodland Cemetery
  Amber Rose European Restaurant

Amber Rose
European Restaurant
DAYTON

THE WONDERFUL OLD WORLD CUISINE WOULD BE REASON ENOUGH to visit the Amber Rose European Restaurant in northeast Dayton. The cabbage rolls are the best I've ever tasted, except, of course, for those my mother makes. Their pierogies are the best I've ever tasted, except, of course, for those my mother makes. The restaurant's turtle soup, made with real turtle, is the best I've ever tasted, except—actually, Mom never made turtle soup. But there is even more incentive to visit the restaurant than just these delicacies: the ghost of Chickie Kseizopolski.

Amber Rose is situated in a quiet residential area, a neighborhood of modest, older homes. Two kids on bikes pedaled up the street as I pulled into the parking lot. A chain-link fence surrounds the backyard of the house adjacent to the lot. In the yard, a little girl was picking daffodils. Two huge plaster geese watched over her. For some reason the geese were painted blue, black, and gray, imitating the colors of no goose ever found in nature.

A brisk spring breeze blew through the lot and clouds scudded overhead. The weather would warm up soon enough, and I imagined neighbors turning out to gossip over fences or on porch steps, just like they probably did years ago when Eastern European immigrant families called the neighborhood home.

In those days, the building that now houses the restaurant was a general store run by Sigmunt Kseizopolski. His wares were displayed behind the large plate glass windows from which diners now survey the passing scene outside. The scale Sigmunt used every day is on display in the restaurant, his name proudly embossed upon it.

The store was more than just a business. It served as something of a community center for the neighborhood's Polish population. On any given day, one could find some of the local gents playing cards or trying their hand at the bowling alley in the basement. The women would come together to exchange news and recipes while they shopped.

Sigmunt and his wife raised six children, and the family lived on the second floor. The store was a family business, with the children helping out until they were old enough to make their own way in the world. The youngest daughter, nicknamed Chickie, never married and lived above the store all her life. By all accounts, she was a happy woman who loved the store and played an active part in running it. Perhaps that is why she still makes her presence known.

"We think she doesn't like the changes that have been made," said Emily Bardonaro, one of Amber Rose's waitresses. "Her little pranks are her way of letting us know."

The restaurant has only been in operation for fourteen years in the century-old building—and, no doubt, in Chickie's memories the place is still a store. I guessed that the wood floors were probably original, as were the sculpted tin ceiling and ceiling fans. The windows could have been the original display windows, although I was not sure about the stained glass panels above each of them. But the long bar, the wooden booths, and the tables covered with floral-print tablecloths would have all been unfamiliar to Chickie. Worse, the second floor where her family had lived had been converted into an additional dining room. Chickie would be very confused when she tried to find her bedroom after a hard day of ghosting.

"What kinds of things have happened?" I asked Emily.

"Dishes have fallen by themselves and sometimes she'll pull glasses down. But the weirdest thing that happened to me was in the storeroom. We used to get these big gallon jars of dressing, and once when I was in there one of the jars fell off the shelf, like it jumped off all by itself. It was a big jar. It didn't just fall."

Emily was young, early twenties maybe, but in the ten minutes I had known her, she didn't seem to me to be a woman easily impressed by such behavior. I wondered if there was more she hadn't told me.

"Have you ever seen the ghost?" I asked.

"No, but my husband has. He used to work here, too. He was working upstairs one night when he saw it. A ball of blue light. At first he thought maybe it was lightning. From where he was standing a window was visible, just on the other side of a doorway, so his first thought was that he had seen lightning through the window. The only problem was that the door was closed so he couldn't have seen the window. The blue light had been there in the room with him."

Emily had briefed me on Chickie's history earlier, consulting every now and then with another waitress and Sue Anne Berry, the manager on duty, to confirm or clarify some of the details. Sue Anne came over to the booth were I sat talking with Emily. Taking a cue from Emily's ghost-light story, Sue Anne told me one of her own.

"Some of the neighbors across the street told us that they had seen lights moving in the windows of the attic. This was after we had closed for the night. They suggested we check the lights to see if they were working correctly, but there are no lights in the attic, so I don't know what they saw."

Sue Anne told me that she, too, had experienced objects moving or falling, seemingly of their own accord. "It's a little spooky at first," she said. "Some of the girls won't go into the basement alone."

"I won't," Emily said, shaking her head.

"The scariest thing that happened to me," Sue Anne continued, "was with the dishwashing machine. There was only one other girl on that night. We were alone in the restaurant and had just about finished cleaning up, when all of a sudden the door on the dishwasher flew up. We both jumped. The door is a big one and has to be pulled down to shut and pulled up to open. It's heavy. There's no way that door could have just opened up like that by itself."

"What did you do?"

"We just got out of there as quick as we could."

I thought about this as I ate my dinner and wondered what I would have done. Yes, I probably would have jumped out of my skin if something like that had happened to me, but all in all Chickie didn't sound particularly malevolent. The atmosphere I felt in the restaurant was not one of dread or fear. On the contrary, it was a warm and inviting kind of place. A family place. Maybe Chickie was just looking for some attention.

After dinner Emily showed me the second floor. The dining room there was bright and cheerful, and try as I might, I just could not sense any negative feelings. Emily showed me the area in which her husband had been working the night he saw the ghost light. The small spare room was an employee work area. Although lacking in drama, and not as cozy as the public areas of the restaurant, it seemed like a normal room. Nothing unusual about it that I could see, but that was then; I wasn't there the night the mystery lights made their dazzling debut.

When we walked back into the dining room, Sue Anne was there. I looked around one last time.

"This is where the family lived," I said, to no one in particular, perhaps thinking that by declaring the fact aloud I would receive some verification from the spirit world.

Nothing.

"Chickie lived here all her life," Sue Anne said. "She loved this place."

"I think she probably did," I said. "And it doesn't seem like she harbors any ill will."

"Oh, no, I don't think so," said Sue Anne. "She just likes to play her little tricks now and then, but that's all."

"You get used to her after awhile," Emily said.

"It's like she's part of the family," added Sue Anne.

"Or it's like you're part of *her* family," I said. "After all, she was here first."

Cincinnati Art Museum

CINCINNATI

JUST AS THE CINCINNATI ART MUSEUM CONTAINS TREASURES FROM ANTIQUITY TO MODERN TIMES gathered from all around the world, the ghosts that roam its cavernous halls after the lights are out are equally international and timeless. The Egyptian mummy. The medieval Spanish monk. The Victorian-era artist. Security guards and mainte- nance workers at the museum have seen these three, along with other unidentifiable entities, haunting the museum.

The beautiful neoclassic edifice stands on a hill in Cincinnati's Eden Park, and houses the Cincinnati Art Academy as well as the museum. Since its founding in 1881, museum curators have collected an eclectic mix of artwork, more than eighty thousand pieces displayed in eighty-eight galleries, providing the residents of Cincinnati with a broad overview of art history.

One of the most popular attractions at the museum, especially among school-age children, is the Egyptian mummy lying in a glass case located in the first-floor antiquities section. An x-ray examination has revealed that the mummy is that of a man, approximately thirty-five years old. Still tightly wrapped in linen, the mummy wears a painted mask, breastplate, and leg coverings. Despite the children pressing fingerprints onto the glass case as they crowd around him, the mummy rests serenely as the long years roll by.

Or does he?

At least one guard has admitted seeing a strange mist resembling the figure of a person rise up above the case holding the mummy, linger in the air for a few moments, then disappear as suddenly as it appeared.

As I stood there in the brightly lit gallery, looking down at the beautifully painted red, black, and gold mask of the mummy, I was drawn to its enigmatic smile and wondered what secrets it concealed. After all, few cultures had as strong an interest in death and the afterlife as did the ancient Egyptians. Perhaps this particular mummy has learned how to cross over between this world and the next at will.

A different sort of apparition has been seen in the second-floor medieval Spanish section. In a small alcove off one of the larger rooms in the gallery is a reproduction of the twelfth-century chapel from Ermita de San Baudelio in north central Spain. As I entered the alcove, the first thing I noticed was the thirteenth-century wooden tomb effigy of Don Sancho Saiz Carillo lying in a glass case directly before me. Beneath a fresco of a knight on horseback, a hunting falcon perched on his hand, Don Sancho lay peacefully, wearing his crown, his sword ready at his side. To the left of the effigy was a tiny room containing an ornate gilt and paint retablo of Saint Peter created by Lorenzo de Zaragoza in 1400. The chapel was to my right.

A Moorish arch lined with faded frescoes of ibises separated the chapel from the alcove. The chapel itself was dark and gloomy, the only light coming from a narrow slit of a window in the wall above where the altar would have been and from one weak electric light set high up in the masonry of the barrel-vaulted roof. On the wall below the window was painted a grotesque creature. It appeared that its ribs were exposed, revealing long, almost dagger-like bones. The beast had a long neck with no head, but a large round eye mounted at the end of the neck had a wicked beak protruding from it. It looked like some creature from a nightmare, although the interpretive sign beside it noted that the fresco artist had actually painted an ibis. In a strange connection to the mummy in the antiquities gallery, the ibis symbolizes the Egyptian god Thoth, who is himself closely associated with the Book of the Dead, a guide to the afterlife buried with ancient Egyptians. Other frescoes of saints and mounted knights decorated the otherwise barren masonry walls of the chapel.

The temperature in the chapel was much cooler than the rest of the alcove or the larger gallery outside, and the thick masonry walls and floor dampened any sound. It was as quiet as any chapel should be, as quiet as a tomb. I stood beneath the arch, the coldest spot in the room, with the gloom of the chapel swirling up behind me as palpable as wind. It was precisely in that spot that the monk had been seen. A seven-foot-tall monk.

One night, as a security guard was making his final rounds of the medieval gallery, he glanced down the gallery toward the alcove and there, standing beneath the Moorish arch, was a robed and hooded figure all in black. The guard froze. He could not make out a face, if indeed the figure had a face. For what seemed like hours, but was in reality only a few moments, the guard stood there unable to move, unable to speak, mesmerized by the towering figure beneath the arch. Then, as he watched in amazement, the hooded apparition slowly began to rise straight up into the air until it disappeared through the ceiling.

The guard never saw the monk again, but Rachel*, another guard, said she is not at all surprised by what her co-worker had seen. "I hear footsteps all the time when I'm closing up for the night," Rachel said, "and I'm always alone. There's never any-one else around. I've heard a lot of stories about the museum's ghosts, and I don't go into the chapel anymore."

Who is the monk? One can only guess. Since he haunts the chapel, perhaps he is some sort of guardian spirit that came with the sacred frescoes from Spain to protect them. Or per-haps he is simply a lost soul, confusing the chapel reproduction with the real thing, the Spanish chapel in which his funeral service was held so many centuries ago.

There is yet another ghost story from the Cincinnati Art Museum, one that appropriately speaks both of the ghost's love of art and of her love for her artist husband, Frank Duveneck. In the Cincinnati Wing of the museum, a small gallery contains a funerary memorial to Elizabeth Boott Duveneck, or "Lizzie," as family and friends knew her. The black plaster effigy is a copy of the original bronze that lies atop her sarcophagus in Allori Cemetery in Florence, Italy. Lizzie rests peacefully, her head lying on a pillow, flowing drapery covering her body as though she were sleeping in bed. She wears a high-collared blouse typical of the 1880s and her hair is plaited in a thick braid coiled upon her head. Her youthful face is serene and at peace with her premature demise. Her hands are folded upon her chest and a large palm frond, symbolizing triumph over death, lies across her body.

The writer Henry James, who was a family friend to Lizzie, traveled to Florence to visit her grave. In a letter to her father he wrote, "One sees, in its place and its ambience, what a meaning and eloquence the whole thing has—and one is touched to tears by this particular example which comes home to one so—of the jolly great truth that it is art alone that triumphs over fate."

If James is right, then it is art alone that keeps Lizzie forever attached to the museum and the Cincinnati Art Academy, which her husband directed from 1909–1915.

Lizzie first met Frank Duveneck at an exhibition of his paintings in Boston. He was everything she was not. While she was the educated, wealthy daughter of a proper Bostonian family, Frank Duveneck was born in Covington, Kentucky, in 1848 to Catholic German immigrants who operated a beer garden. A true starving artist, Duveneck had a natural talent for painting and, at twenty-one, was able to study at a prestigious art academy in Munich, Germany.

By the time Duveneck was teaching his own students in Munich, Lizzie and her widowed father were living in Florence, Italy, at Villa Castellani. They decided to join Duveneck's students in Munich. While Lizzie's father could appreciate Duveneck's artistry and teaching abilities, these qualities alone were not enough to recommend the artist as a match for his daughter. Still, even though the German-accented Duveneck was two years younger than Lizzie and of a lower social class, she was taken in by his charm, his jokes, and his good nature.

To one of her friends Lizzie wrote, "We found him and were pleased. He is a remarkable looking young man, and a gentleman, which I did not expect. He has a fine head and a keen eye and the perceptions strongly developed."

In 1880 they decided to marry but soon broke off the engagement as Lizzie's desire to be a professional painter clashed with her feelings for her teacher. She was ambitious; he was lazy. Her life with her father was one of sophisticated solitude. With Duveneck it was crude, loud, yet generous. Issues of money and class surfaced in their relationship, which became the inspiration for James's novel, *Portrait of a Lady*.

Love won out in the end. In 1886, just a few months shy of her fortieth birthday, Lizzie and Frank Duveneck were married—but not before Lizzie's father made his new son-in-law sign an agreement that would deny him any inheritance in the event of his wife's death. In 1887, a son was born to the couple, and Lizzie's father reinstated his son-in-law's inheritance rights.

By 1888, the Duveneck family was living in Paris, where Frank reconnected with some of his Munich artist colleagues. Now burdened with a child, husband, and elderly father, Lizzie did not find Paris life exactly what she had expected. Her artistic ambitions suffered. Still, she managed to submit her watercolors side-by-side with her husband's paintings to the jury for the 1888 Paris Salon.

On the day that the jury voted, Lizzie went to bed, sick with a chill. Four days later she died of pneumonia.

Frank Duveneck returned to the United States the following year, left his son in the care of his in-laws in Boston, and settled in Cincinnati. There he began the memorial to the love of his life, a woman to whom he had been married only two years. Lizzie's effigy was the first sculptural piece Duveneck had ever attempted, so he enlisted the aid of Clement J. Barnhorn, a local sculptor. The simple but elegant effigy was awarded an honorable mention by the Paris Salon of 1895, and a copy was exhibited in the Boston Museum of Fine Art where Frank and Lizzie's son could view it.

Frank Duveneck lived out his life in Cincinnati, where he was named to the faculty of the Cincinnati Academy of Art and eventually served as its director. He died in 1919 and was buried across the Ohio River in his hometown of Covington, Kentucky.

And Lizzie still "resides" nearby.

A wispy dark mist has been seen rising up from the effigy, coalescing into a human-like shape as it hovers over the recumbent figure of Lizzie. It floats there only seconds before vanishing into the air. Perhaps Lizzie is searching for Frank, waiting for him to rejoin her, surrounded by the art they both so loved.

"Why not?" said Don*, the guard on duty the day I visited the Cincinnati Wing of the museum. "They had a real love story going, just like in the movies. Maybe it never ends."

Cincinnati Music Hall

CINCINNATI

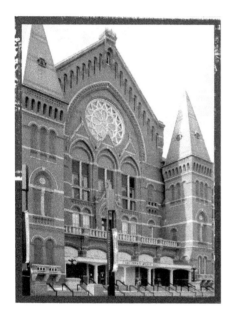

MUSIC HATH CHARMS TO SOOTHE THE SAVAGE BEAST.
If music can, indeed, calm the hearts of wild animals, might
it not also calm the restless spirits of those who have died and
wander the earth as ghosts? I could think of no better place to
find the answer to that question than Cincinnati Music Hall.

Built in 1878, the red-brick, Victorian Gothic structure rises ma-
jestically on the corner of 14th and Elm streets. Central Park-way
runs parallel to the rear of the building now, but when Music Hall
first opened its doors that thoroughfare was actually the Miami
Canal. Designed by a local architectural firm, the edifice is an architectural eccentricity with its garrets, turrets, gables, insets, nooks,

broken surfaces and planes, and ornate rose window. Some witty Cincinnatians have dubbed the style "Sauerbraten Byzantine."

The building is located upon the site where the tin-roofed wooden Sangerhalle once stood, a hall built by a German immigrant singing society, the Saengerbund, for its May Festivals. But there is also a more somber atmosphere associated with other former occupants of the site. The present Music Hall rests upon the foundations of the 1844 Orphan Asylum. Before that was the Commercial Hospital and Lunatic Asylum with its Pest House, a section for the indigent with contagious diseases. A potter's field also occupied the site, the final resting place for suicides and strangers, the indigent and homeless of Cincinnati, and those who died in the Pest House. These unfortunates were buried without the benefit of coffins; they were simply bundled up and dropped into the earth. Over the years, there have been many renovations to Music Hall, and human bones have often been unearthed during construction.

The famous Cincinnati journalist Lafcadio Hearn wrote about one such discovery in the October 22, 1876, edition of the *Cincinnati Commercial:*

> This rich yellow soil, fat with the human flesh and bone and brain it has devoured, is being disemboweled by a hundred spades and forced to exhibit its ghastly secrets to the sun . . . you will behold small Golgothas—mingled with piles of skulls, loose vertebrae, fibulas, tibias and the great curving bones of the thigh . . . All are yellow, like the cannibal clay which denuded them of their fleshly masks . . . Bone after bone . . . is turned over with a scientific application of kicks . . . dirty fingers are poked into empty eyesockets . . . ribs crack in pitiful remonstrance to reckless feet; and tobacco juice is carelessly squirted among the decaying skulls . . . by night there come medical students to steal the poor skulls.

Hearn reported that the dead soon began to make themselves known to the living just shortly after these macabre discoveries were made. Shadowy figures roamed the halls at night and ghostly dancers were seen in the ballroom on the second floor. One exhibitor at a business fair in Music Hall saw a young, pale woman in old-fashioned clothing standing by his booth. As he approached her, he felt a sudden rush of cold air as the figure became transparent, then disappeared. Hearn wrote: "The tall woman had been sepulchered under the yellow clay below the planking upon which he stood; and the worms had formed the wedding-rings of Death about her fingers half a century before."

Half a dozen skeletons were unearthed by workers in 1927, placed in a cement crypt, and reburied, only to be discovered again during a renovation in 1969. The bones were placed inside another concrete box and reburied—and uncovered in 1988 for the third time when the shaft for the concert hall's freight elevator was deepened. It seems the dead at Music Hall simply cannot rest in peace. Pieces, yes, but peace? No.

When my wife, Mary, and I lived in the Cincinnati area we attended several performances of various kinds at Music Hall, but that was before we had ever heard the ghost stories, and we had never been behind the scenes. We were lucky enough, however, on a recent Valentine's Day to have a tour of Music Hall led by Marie Gallagher, a volunteer there for twenty-five years. It was a public tour, and we were joined by approximately two dozen people who were interested in seeing the grand old building. We gathered in the main foyer, with its checkerboard marble floor and graceful columns.

Marie knew every nook and cranny of Music Hall and regaled us with tales and anecdotes about some of the famous people who had performed there—John Philip Sousa, Richard Strauss, Igor Stravinsky, Leonard Bernstein, Jascha Heifitz, Maria Callas,

Andres Segovia, Luciano Pavarotti, Count Basie, Miles Davis, Bob Dylan—the list is endless.

The heart and soul of Music Hall is the 3,630-seat Springer Auditorium. Marie led us up into the gallery where we could look down at the burgundy-colored seats and the stage. Even though larger than most concert halls, the acoustics in Springer Auditorium are said to be the best in the country, if not the world. Ed Vignale, Jr., Music Hall's facilities engineer, told me in a later conversation that a person standing in the gallery of the empty auditorium could hear someone speaking from behind the stage as though he or she were only twenty feet away from the listener. Could it be that such perfect acoustics are the explanation for some of the ghostly sounds heard at Music Hall?

"I hear them when I'm on duty alone at night," said Kitty Love, who has been part of the private police force at Music Hall for twenty-one years. "Footsteps, doors slamming, and music playing, and I know I was the only one in the building."

Kitty has heard the footsteps and slamming doors in the stage area of Springer Auditorium and in other parts of the building's south side, the side that was built over the cemetery.

Now, as our tour group stood in the gallery of the auditorium, gazing out at the magnificent 1,500-pound crystal chandelier suspended from the dome ceiling and its Arthur Thompson oil painting, "Allegory of the Arts," I thought of what Kitty had said and took a few pictures with my digital camera. Later, when I download the images to my computer, I will find three beautiful but unexplainable orbs floating in the otherwise clear air above the gallery.

Marie continued to lead us on the tour—the enormous backstage area with its vertiginous catwalks barely distinguishable in the darkness high above us, the massive workshop where stage sets and props are built, the costume room with its many rows of clothes of every description and time period hung

around and above us like an enormous dry cleaner, the dressing rooms that resembled high school locker rooms, and the
more luxuriously appointed dressing rooms of the stars.

When the tour concluded back in the main foyer, Marie took
us aside privately and brought us back into an office area. In this
section was a freight elevator, the very elevator beneath which a
small casket of bones from the old cemetery was uncovered.

"I haven't seen or heard anything unusual in Music Hall and
I don't believe in ghosts," said Marie, "but this is where a security guard said he heard strange music. He was so impressed by
what he heard, he wrote it all down."

She handed me a file folder containing a photocopy of security
guard John G. Engst's handwritten account of what he experienced on February 22, 1987. In it he tells how he was escorting
three caterers from a party held in Music Hall's Corbett Tower
down to the first floor in the elevator. It was about 12:30 A.M. As
they descended, the three women asked him if he heard music.
He said he did not, but they asked him again when they reached
the first floor and this time he said he heard it. The women told
John they had heard the same music when they went up to
Corbett Tower a few hours earlier but didn't think much of it then.

After the women loaded their truck and drove away, John
went back to the elevator. The music, sounding something like
a music box, continued to play a tune that John thought he
recognized as "Let Me Call You Sweetheart." John stopped the
elevator at different levels to see if the music would still be audible. It was. He wrote, "It was as beautiful as ever, but I'm getting
more bewildered."

John checked all the areas outside the elevator at the various
levels, but could not find any source for the music. He was so
frightened and awed by his experience that he wrote, "For
nearly two weeks I could not approach the elevator shaft on the
first floor late at night without my whole body tingling."

In the final analysis, however, the experience was an affirming, life-altering one for John Engst. He wrote: "The experience is now all positive and will be forever, I now believe. I pray more intensely, don't fear death and am glad to have had this profound experience."

Kitty Love has heard similar ghostly music at Music Hall, but in different locations than the freight elevator. "You hear music playing somewhere late at night when you know no one is there, but when you get there, you find it coming from some other place. You go to that place and then you hear it coming from yet another place."

Ed Vignale said a musical greeting card had been found at the bottom of the elevator shaft, but that didn't convince Engst that there was a rational explanation for the music he heard. Maybe John is right. Those greeting cards don't usually last very long, nor do they play continuously. Once opened they play only a few seconds before they must be closed and reopened to play again. Could a card have been heard continuously for several hours? And what about the ethereal music Kitty heard in other parts of Music Hall? Are there ghosts roaming Music Hall?

Even though Ed Vignale said that he has never seen or heard spirits in the thirty-four years he has worked at Music Hall, he admits that some people have told him of seeing men and women dressed in late nineteenth-century clothing walking through the halls of the building. Other people have said that sometimes an extra, unknown "cast member" may appear in an operatic production, or that unusual-looking figures may appear among the audience.

"There is definitely something strange going on here," Ed said. "In all the time I've worked here, I've only seen two mice and one rat in the building, very unusual for a building of this size and age." Ed went on to say that during a 1967 production at Music Hall called Wild Animal Cargo, two baby snakes, a python and boa constrictor, somehow disappeared and were never found. The show left town without them and Music Hall was left with a unique system of rodent extermination.

Orbs in Cincinnati Music Hall's Springer Auditorium.

How long do those snakes live anyway? One can only hope that if they are still alive those creatures have long ago been tamed by the musical charms of Cincinnati Music Hall's resident spirits.

Heritage Village Museum

SHARON WOODS, SHARONVILLE

Hayner House,
circa 1852, Heritage
Village Museum.

I'VE KNOWN LONNA KINGSBURY FOR ALMOST A
DECADE, and if she says a place is haunted, I believe her. Lonna
is an artist, actress, and writer who has been involved with many
arts projects in the Cincinnati area over the years. One of her current projects is an acting role. She plays Catherine Coffin, the wife
of abolitionist Levi Coffin, in a production at Heritage Village
called *Cincinnati's Runaway Slave*. The drama, now in its fourth
year, tells the stories of the escaped slaves who made their way to
freedom during the Civil War via the Underground Railroad, and
the people, such as the real-life Coffins, who aided them along the
way. Catherine Coffin hid runaway slaves in the cellar of her house.

There could be no better location for the production of the play than Heritage Village Museum, located in Sharon Woods Park in Sharonville. Here, eleven authentic nineteenth-century buildings have been collected from all around Ohio, re-creating a village complete with a church, doctor's office, general store, railroad station, and several homes of different styles. The *Runaway Slave* drama moves from building to building, completely engaging the audience in the drama.

In September 2002, Lonna was at a play rehearsal at Heritage Village. The cast was assembled in the church, which is at one end of the village. Lonna was to be interviewed on television the next morning in costume, so she left rehearsal early and made her way to the Hayner House, where the costumes were stored.

"It was dark," Lonna said, "and the Hayner House was way at the other end of the village. I could see the white columns in front of the house dimly glowing in the distance."

Lonna was alone as she crossed the village and stepped up onto the porch of the Hayner House.

I had visited Heritage Village many times in the past, especially during Christmas, when the village is decked out in its holiday finery and hot cider and cookies can be found in the Hayner House. At those times, the Victorian-style house would be ablaze with lights and decorated with ribbons, bows, and Christmas trees.

But I had never been there alone on a chilly September night, when the house probably looked more like something out of a Charles Addams cartoon than it did a welcoming abode from Dickens's *A Christmas Carol*. I could imagine Lonna fumbling with the key in the dark as she unlocked the door.

"I've been in and out of that place so many times that I know my way around by heart," Lonna said. "I wasn't afraid."

She had been told by someone in the cast that her costume was hanging in a closet in the center room on the ground floor.

She didn't bother with a light since she knew her way around so well. When she opened the closet, her costume wasn't there.

"I stood there for a moment, wondering where else it could be, and that's when I heard the sounds," Lonna said. "I heard party talk, voices and laughter. I heard the clinking of glasses.

"My first thought was not of ghosts. I just thought people were in the house having a party. I turned on the lights. I could still hear the party sounds, so I went to check it out."

Lonna went from room to room, flicking on lights as she went, but she could not find anyone. Still, the laughter and voices persisted.

"Now I was sure that someone was playing a joke on me, someone from the cast. I was calling, 'Come on, guys, come on out,' as I went around the house, but nobody showed up. I could still hear the sounds. I went through the entire house. Nothing. Yet, there was a party going on that I wasn't privy to. Finally, I went back to the front door and stepped out on the porch. There was no one outside the house either, and that's when the realization that I had actually been alone all the time hit me. I went back inside for a moment, but there was only silence. The party was over. At the other end of the village the other cast members were still at the church, but here I was entirely alone."

Sometime later, Lonna told the others what had happened to her at the Hayner House. They all denied any knowledge of the event, but none of them were at all surprised.

"You have to remember that all the buildings at the village came from somewhere else and that each of them have their own particular histories," Lonna said. "Who knows what happened inside them or what stories they could tell?"

Lonna said that other people working at or visiting the Hayner House have felt cold spots in the upstairs offices that cannot be attributed to air conditioning or drafts. Psychic researchers recognize such cold spots as evidence of a ghostly presence. It is also not unusual for the lights at Hayner House to turn themselves off and on at will. Electrical disturbances are also associated with ghosts who may "feed" off electrical sources.

People have also heard footsteps walking back and forth on the second floor of Elklick house, the house that is used to portray the Coffin house in the *Runaway Slave* production.

"There is one man in the cast who won't go inside Elklick house unless someone is already inside or goes with him. He'll wait outside the house until someone shows up," Lonna said.

No one knows the identity of the ghosts that may be producing these phenomena in Heritage Village, nor has anyone yet attempted to research the ghostly history of the various buildings. Since ghosts frequently become active when their environments are damaged or altered in some way, especially through renovations or remodeling, there could very well be ghosts at the village. After all, how disrupting would it be to have your home ripped off its foundation, with you in it, and hauled many miles away to be turned into a museum?

The Golden Lamb Inn

LEBANON

WHEN JONAS SEAMAN MIGRATED FROM NEW JERSEY TO OHIO IN 1803 and opened The Golden Lamb Inn on Broadway in the newly-platted village of Lebanon, he could never have imagined that more than two hundred years later his establishment would still be offering food and lodging for weary travelers. Nor could he have imagined that some of his guests, even after so long a period of time, would still be there.

But they are.

Much has been written about The Golden Lamb, and for good reason. The whole parade of American history not only passed by the inn's doors, it stopped to rest awhile. The inn has hosted ten

U.S. presidents: John Quincy Adams, Van Buren, both Benjamin and William Henry Harrison, Grant, McKinley, Hayes, Garfield, Taft, and Harding. Other notables who have stayed there include: DeWitt Clinton, Henry Clay, Daniel Webster, Horace Mann, Harriett Beecher Stowe, Clement Vallandigham, William Dean Howells, Cordell Hull, Mark Twain, Charles Dickens, and James Whitcomb Riley.

Some of these people have left more than just their signatures in the guest register. Their spirits still occupy the rooms of The Golden Lamb.

One such spirit is that of Clement L. Vallandigham, a celebrated U.S. congressman from Ohio during the Civil War. Vallandigham rose to fame as the leader of the Peace Democrats, a group that in 1863 issued a statement declaring that the war "against the South is illegal, unconstitutional, and should not be sustained." The Peace Democrats, and other anti-war groups collectively called "copperheads," were seen by the government as obstacles to the war effort, and every attempt was made to silence them.

General Ambrose Burnside, commanding the Department of the Ohio, issued a general order that any person committing "expressed or implied" treason would be subject to a military court and could be punished by death or banishment. His first test case was Vallandigham.

Shortly after he gave an inflammatory speech in Mount Vernon, Ohio, on May 1, 1863, a party of soldiers came to Vallandigham's house in Dayton in the middle of the night, knocked down the door, and dragged him away, leaving behind his hysterical wife and sister-in-law. His arrest set off violent civil rights protests; his supporters rioted in the streets and burned down the offices of Dayton's Republican newspaper.

In Cincinnati, a military court found Vallandigham guilty of "having expressed sympathy" for the enemy and having uttered "disloyal sentiments and opinions." President Abraham Lincoln, embarrassed by the public furor over the Vallandigham case but unwilling to undermine one of his generals, supported Vallandigham's banishment rather than death by firing squad. On May 25 a contingent of Union cavalrymen under a flag of truce escorted Vallandigham to Confederate General Braxton Bragg's lines south of Murfreesboro, Tennessee.

All this time, Vallandigham had been campaigning for the Ohio governorship. After his banishment he managed to eventually sail to Canada, where he continued his campaign from exile, though unsuccessfully. In 1864, he returned to Ohio unmolested.

The Vallandigham Dining Room is a small parlor on the second floor of The Golden Lamb. Long white curtains were pulled back from the single window overlooking the street. A large table surrounded by six chairs was set with a snowy white tablecloth. A colorful flower arrangement rested on the table. A fireplace was set against the far wall and near it, hung against the red floral print wallpaper, was a portrait of Clement L. Vallandigham. He gazed out at me from the gilded frame, a handsome man with a full head of hair and a luxurious moustache. The curtains reflected in the glass covering the portrait draped over his head like a shroud.

It was in this room that Vallandigham accidentally shot himself to death. In the hall outside the door there is a framed newspaper account of his tragic-comic death. Years after his return to Ohio and his failed run for the governorship, Vallandigham was a practicing lawyer. He was in Lebanon representing a man named McGeehan, accused of shooting another man, named Meyers, to death. Vallandigham's defense rested on the premise that the dead man had actually shot himself unintentionally.

Vallandigham was discussing the case with his associate, an attorney named McBurney. A local newspaper tells what happened on that night, June 16, 1871. Vallandigham "picked up a revolver and putting it in his right pocket, drew it out far enough only to keep the muzzle touching his body and snapped the hammer. The weapon exploded and sent its deadly missile into the abdomen at a point almost corresponding with that in which Meyers was shot. Mr. Vallandigham exclaimed that he had taken up the wrong pistol."

Apparently, Vallandigham had two pistols on the table, one loaded, the other unloaded and, in his excitement to demonstrate to McBurney how Meyers could have killed himself, grabbed the wrong gun. Vallandigham's 9 P.M. telegraph to his doctor is both poignant and stoic: "Dr. Reeve—I shot myself by accident with a pistol in the bowels. I fear I am fatally injured. Come at once. —C.L. Vallandigham." He died at the inn the following morning.

Vallandigham's ghost is a regular at The Golden Lamb.

De-De Bailey, a manager at the inn who has worked there for twenty-seven years, told me that his profile once appeared in a window in a photo taken upstairs.

"It was very clear," she said. "You could see his eyes, nose, his moustache. It was definitely him."

The Golden Lamb's
Vallandigham Dining Room,
where his portrait still hangs
on the wall.

This is no small admission for De-De. In all her years at the inn, she had never seen a ghost, nor witnessed any ghostly activities, until only a few weeks before I paid my visit to the inn.

"Of course, I knew all the stories and I knew that many people had seen ghosts here, but I was always skeptical. Until now," she said.

She told me that she had been talking with one of the servers in a dining room on the ground floor. She walked away from the server and was at the opposite end of the room when she clearly heard a deep sigh behind her.

"I turned around fast because it scared me, but there was no one there. The server hadn't seen or heard anything, but I know what I heard. It was a human sound, maybe a man. After all these years something finally happened to me. I couldn't believe it."

De-De thought that maybe the ghosts were worried about the repairs going on at the inn. Only a month or so before, a roofing contractor had piled up too much roofing material in one spot on the old roof and part of it collapsed. It wasn't the ten-foot hole left in the roof that damaged the inn as much as the water that the hole let in. The inn was only closed a few days, but repairs were still going on, and De-De thought they upset the ghosts.

"They're used to being closed in here. Maybe they're telling us how much they don't like being exposed," she said.

That could be. Ghosts are often agitated when buildings are renovated, damaged, or remodeled. Paranormal activity always seems to increase in such circumstances. That heightened activity may explain why De-De was only now experiencing paranormal events, though the inn has long been haunted.

Was that sighing the voice of Clement Vallandigham's ghost? It's possible, especially since he's actually been seen at the inn. A server reported seeing a man dressed in old-fashioned clothes and wearing a "tall hat"—possibly an 1860s style stovepipe hat—in the Corwin Dining Room on the second floor, and a housekeeper said she saw a man matching that description sitting on a bench in the hall on the fourth floor. Both descriptions of the man strongly resemble Vallandigham.

Some people claim, however, that the male ghost may be that of Ohio Supreme Court Justice Charles R. Sherman, the father of Civil War General William T. Sherman. Justice Sherman died suddenly at the inn at the age of forty-one, leaving his wife and eleven children penniless. As a result, most of the children were put up for adoption. Such guilt would lie heavily on a man's soul and might cause him to remain earthbound, forever seeking forgiveness.

As I was talking to De-De in the lobby of The Golden Lamb, some of the other staff members gathered around. It was a warm and sunny Sunday morning and most of the guests had already checked out. The restaurant was not yet open for lunch, so things were quiet. The stories started coming fast and furious.

De-De told me that one night auditors saw a little girl on the staircase right there in the lobby—and she suddenly disappeared. Another auditor had seen several chairs in the closed dining room suddenly fall over at the same time.

Cherie came up from the inn's gift shop in the basement and stood behind the counter, listening.

"Would you like to hear a gift shop story?" she asked. She told me that one of the employees seemed to attract spirits in the gift shop. Several times, a row of stuffed animals would throw themselves off the shelf at her.

"I don't just mean one or two animals. I mean the whole shelf," Cherie said. "They would actually leap off the shelf at her when she went by. I saw it once for myself. I couldn't believe my eyes."

I shuddered at the thought, remembering the gruesome television show *When Stuffed Animals Attack*.

"There's more," Cherie said. "One day I was talking to a customer about the ghosts and I told her that I didn't really believe in them. Just when I said that, the cash register started up all by itself and spat out this crazy receipt, nothing but "X"s and "O"s, gibberish. I showed it to the manager and he didn't know what to make of it."

Geri Wilson was running a vacuum by the counter when she joined in the conversation. She turned off the vacuum to tell me about her encounter with the ghost of Sarah, or at least with one of Sarah's family members. Geri had been cleaning rooms on the fourth floor, the floor where most ghostly events occur.

"There was no one else on the floor but me and I heard a man's voice call, 'Sarah!' It was a deep, authoritative voice, and for some reason I was certain it was the voice of Sarah's grandfather," she said. "I don't know why I felt that, but I was sure it was him."

Sarah was the daughter of Albert and Eunice Stubbs. Albert died when Sarah was just a child, and her mother moved them into The Golden Lamb, which had recently come under the ownership of her brother-in-law, Isaac Stubbs, who purchased the inn in 1841. They lived on the second floor in what is now the Presidential Dining Room. Sarah lived at the inn for several years, grew up, and had a family of her own, eventually dying in old age. Some people believe that it is Sarah who haunts the inn as a little girl.

Today, Sarah's childhood rocker and a small table she owned are displayed in a little room called Sarah's Room. Later, when I went upstairs, I stopped at Sarah's Room, which is now kept as a museum to the memory of a long-ago childhood. Looking through the window in the door to the room, I saw a small child's bed with an old-fashioned dress laid carefully upon it, a sled, a doll crib, dolls, and other toys.

Geri also told me about another housekeeper working on the fourth floor who heard what she described as the sound of a tricycle in the hall and heard a little voice call out, "Sarah's back." She rushed out into the hall, but there was no one there.

There is another theory as to the identity of the little girl ghost. In 1825, noted orator and politician Henry Clay was traveling through the area with his wife, Lucretia, and Eliza, their youngest daughter. Clay, who was at that time President John Quincy Adams's Secretary of State, was on his way to Washington. Eliza fell ill during the trip and the family found lodgings at The Golden Lamb. A doctor was summoned, and he said that the little girl was too sick to travel. The family remained in Lebanon for several weeks until the doctor finally declared that little Eliza would, in fact, recover fully.

With the duties of his cabinet position pressing upon him, Clay departed for Washington, not without concern about leaving his daughter and wife at the inn. He was less than twenty miles from the capitol when he read in a newspaper that his daughter had died. The little girl was buried in a local cemetery, and the heart-broken Lucretia returned to the Clay home in Lexington, Kentucky, alone. It wasn't until the 1890s that descendants of Henry Clay finally brought the girl's remains home to the family burial plot in Kentucky.

So, it could very well be that little Eliza is still a presence at The Golden Lamb. And maybe she has company. Maybe there are two little girl ghosts, keeping each other company, playing hide-and-seek in the dark and silent hallways of the inn.

I wandered the different guest floors, peering into the unmade rooms, each of which bore the name of a famous inn guest. There were only a few other housekeepers on duty besides Geri, so the floors were mostly empty as I explored them. There was something melancholy about looking into these dim rooms, full of brooding antique furniture, and seeing the disarrayed bedcovers. In the absence of any persons in the room, one could imagine that there had been no guests at all, at least no flesh-and-blood guests. It could just as easily have been the ghosts of the inn who had slept there, comfortable in death as they had been in life.

I saw Geri sitting on the carpeted stairs between floors. She was waiting for the last guests to check out before making up their room. I sat beside her on the steps.

We talked some more about ghosts and she told me a few stories she had heard from her native Louisiana. Geri was sixty-eight years old but hadn't worked at the inn all that long. Still, in a short period of time, she had had her share of paranormal events. In addition to hearing the voice, she has also heard doors opening and closing in empty rooms on the fourth floor.

"Have you ever experienced these kinds of things before in your life?" I asked.

"No. I'm a born-again Christian," she said. "And I know people say I shouldn't believe in them, but what are you going to do? They're here." She shook her head slowly. "They're here."

Hilton Cincinnati, Netherland Plaza

CINCINNATI

ONE THING I HAVE DISCOVERED ABOUT GHOSTS WHO HAUNT HOTELS IS THAT THEY HAVE EXCELLENT TASTE. It makes perfect sense to me that "The Lady in Green" would still be searching for her husband after all these years amid the opulent French Art Deco splendor of the Netherland Plaza hotel. Her story is a sad one, the story of a deep love between a woman and a man that even death could not destroy. It is also a story integral to the history of the hotel.

As Chicago architect Walter W. Ahlschlarger conceived it in the 1920s, the hotel was an important part of Carew Tower, an innovative multiple-use complex that combined the hotel and its restaurants, department stores, specialty shops, and parking garage into a "city within a city." Ahlschlager included such modern advancements as indirect lighting systems, internal broadcasting systems, ultra-modern baths (Winston Churchill, a frequent guest at the Netherland Plaza, was so impressed with the bathroom facilities in his suite—now named in his honor—that he had it all copied, down to the last detail, in his own country home in England), high-speed elevators, and a fully automated parking garage in which automobiles literally parked themselves.

The décor of the hotel wedded an Old World atmosphere with the "modernity" of the French Art Deco style, taking its inspiration from Egyptian, Mayan, and Aztec influences. Several areas in the hotel were designed to look almost like Hollywood sets, and visitors today may be reminded of *Indiana Jones*, *The Mummy*, or, as concierge T.J. Mobilio said, *The Shining*.

"The first time I was ever at the hotel I was sitting at the bar, talking with the bartender, and thinking to myself that this place was right out of *The Shining*. I knew then I wanted to work here," he said.

T.J. is right. We were sitting at a small table in the Palm Court, the hotel's restaurant and lounge. Bob Louis, the hotel's director of sales and marketing, had asked T.J to speak with me and fill me in on the ghostly history of the hotel, since T.J. had made himself something of the hotel's unofficial historian.

Large plant-like sconces mounted on dark Brazilian rosewood wall paneling dimly light the huge Palm Court. The soaring ceiling is fashioned in a step pyramid shape and is painted with classical murals in Baroque style, illustrating the theme of re-creation. A mezzanine surrounded the restaurant and I could see an occasional guest walking by beyond the balustrades. Although there were only one or two patrons at the bar situated at the north end of the room, I could easily imagine ghostly partygoers in formal attire enjoying themselves in the cavernous room.

The Palm Court at the Hilton Cincinnati.

"And just like in the movie, there is a ghost, right?" I said.

"Yes, the 'Lady in Green.' I've never seen her, but I know people who have, people who I trust completely and know well."

"What happened?"

"There were a few things," T.J. said. "One of our servers was making a room service run. He got on one of the elevators and there was an African-American woman there wearing a green dress, more like a formal gown actually. As the elevator rose they talked about how nice the Hall of Mirrors looked. The server said they talked for about thirty seconds. Then he looked away for just a moment and when he looked back, she had disappeared. He was so shaken up by the incident that he took two weeks off from work."

"He still works here?" I asked.

"Yes, and he thinks differently about our ghost than he did before."

"When did he see the ghost?"

"A few years ago, but I have even more recent stories. This one was in the last eighteen months. During the week we have a lot of business travelers. One night this stern-looking businessman checks in. He was all business and was tired. He just wanted to go to his room right away. We checked him in and it wasn't forty-five minutes later that he was back down at the front desk wearing only his boxer shorts, a T-shirt, and socks. He was terrified. He wouldn't tell us what was wrong—he just wanted out of the hotel. He wouldn't even go back up for his bags. He never explained it. He just said he was afraid and that was it. He wouldn't go back."

I sat there for a moment looking at T.J., trying to figure out if the young man was perhaps exaggerating—okay, lying—but I didn't think he was. In his gray concierge suit, he looked serious. Plus, he was able to tell me the story with a straight face, although he chuckled at the thought of the stuffy businessman reduced to a blubbering child. I figured T.J. was telling me the truth. I also thought that, scary as the businessman's encounter may have been, how scary would it have been for other hotel guests to see him standing there in his skivvies?

T.J. had another story to tell me.

Airline pilots are frequent guests at downtown Cincinnati hotels, and the Netherland Plaza is home for the pilots and crew of a few airlines. T.J. said that one day one of the pilots came "staggering" out of the elevator and ran to the front desk, saying he had seen a ghost in there with him. At first, the staff though he was drunk, he was shaking so much. After only a few moments, however, they could see that he was sober, though badly shaken.

"He was white as a ghost, if you'll excuse the pun," T.J. said. "He said that he was alone on the elevator when he felt a cold breeze blow across the back of his neck. He turned and saw a lady in a green dress. His description of her matched the server's description to a T. The pilot said that she was there for only a few seconds before she vanished.

"He still stays here when he's in town. I see him often, but he doesn't talk about the incident and we don't ask him."

That night, as I rode the elevator up to my room on the twentieth floor, I was more aware of the air around me than ever before. I was alone and I noticed how the polished wood paneling reflected my image back to me. But any way I looked at it, no matter how much I squinted, I could not change my reflection into an African-American woman in a green ball gown.

I did have my own scary experience on the elevator, however, when I found myself the only male, trapped in the rear of the elevator by a contingent of ample-bosomed, horn-rimmed-glasses-wearing Tupperware salesladies in town for a convention. I still get the shivers thinking about it.

I survived the Tupperware onslaught and met with Carla Ballard, the hotel's senior national account executive, the following day.

"Yes, the Lady in Green has been seen on the elevators, but she is usually in the Hall of Mirrors or right there, on the eastern mezzanine," Carla said, pointing to the balustrade high above where we sat in the Palm Court.

Carla was tall and thin with reddish hair. She wore a black suit and skirt and was simultaneously professional and friendly. She had brought me a packet of information about the hotel, which I leafed through as we spoke.

"Who is the Lady in Green, anyway?" I asked. "Does anyone know?"

"You probably already know that the hotel was built in 1931," Carla said, "but you might not know that the whole thing took only one year to complete. Thousands of laborers worked around the clock everyday to get the job done. As you can imagine, there were some accidents. In one of them, a painter working right here in the Palm Court, which was originally the main lobby, fell to his death. It's said that once the hotel was finished and open for business, the man's widow checked in and threw herself out a window."

"And no one knows her name?"

Carla shook her head. "Nor can we find any historical documentation of her suicide."

Carla also told me the pilot story and her version matched T.J.'s. She also had two stories of her own. She told me about the night auditor who was on one of the guest floors delivering express checkouts. She said that, even though he was all alone in the hall, he suddenly heard a woman's voice say, "Excuse me, can you help me?" He took off running downstairs and immediately quit.

"The poor man almost had a nervous breakdown," Carla said.

She told me about the time one of the hotel's sales consultants was showing a customer the grand ballroom, the Hall of Mirrors.

"The two of them were standing in the balcony overlooking the ballroom, talking about its accommodations. Suddenly, the customer grabbed the consultant's arm and held onto it tightly. 'Did you see that?' she asked the consultant. Apparently, for just a second, the woman caught a glimpse of the ghost in the room."

After talking with Carla I decided to check out the Hall of Mirrors for myself. I went up to the third-floor lobby, then walked up the curving staircase to the ballroom's balcony. Inside, the room was nothing short of palatial.

The balustrade surrounding the balcony was made of German silver—an alloy of copper, zinc, and nickel—and was fashioned into floral garlands and depictions of Pan. Egyptian-style chandeliers hung from the ceiling, surrounding a central mural painted inside a mock dome. Below me, and at the opposite end of the ballroom, was a majestic staircase, backed by an enormous mirror.

There was no one in the ballroom and the lighting, as it is throughout the hotel, was soft and subdued. Romantic in the right circumstances, maybe a bit creepy in others. The light had an amber cast to it, the result of the large mirrors that line the walls in the ballroom and the balcony. The mirrors are backed with 18k gold and are insured with Lloyds of London. It is the gold backing that causes the amber reflection.

The Hall of Mirrors at the Hilton Cincinnati.

I went back downstairs and entered the ballroom from its floor level. There were many tables and chairs in the room, some of them already dressed in white for a wedding reception that would take place there the next day. Despite the size of the room, it was very quiet, still. I walked around, taking my time, letting the aura of the room wash over me. Often I thought I saw someone from the corner of my eye, only to find myself looking at my own reflection, caught in one or more of the many mirrors in the room. Certainly, so many mirrors could be a plausible explanation for seeing ghosts, but as in the elevator, I was seeing myself, not a woman. In fact, the mirrors may be a help to the ghost since so many psychic researchers believe that mirrors may serve as psychic portals to the spirit world.

I didn't see the Lady in Green that day, but I thought of those who had seen her. The pilot, the food server, the customer. Each of them described the woman in the same manner, and each of them referred to her as being as solid as a real person. No wispy mists for this ghost. She wants to be seen. Why else would she wear a green ball gown? Seeing a ghost, an apparition, in such detail—and being able to talk with it, as did the server—is fairly unusual as paranormal events go.

Being touched by such a ghost is even more rare, yet that is what happened to one guest, according to concierge Mariuxi Robles.

"The man was in the hall, looking for his room. There was no one else there. Suddenly, someone tapped him on the shoulder and asked him for help. When he turned around, there was a lady in a green dress. Then she was gone. He wanted his room changed after that."

"Have you ever seen her?" I asked.

"No," she said, "and I don't think I want to, but I think she's here."

"Why?"

"Just a feeling I have," she said. She was standing in the kitchen of the Belvedere Club on the sixteenth floor, talking to me through the serve-through. She was young and pleasant and spoke with a charming Hispanic accent that she had brought with her from her native Ecuador. "I have to come in early to set up the room for breakfast, and I'm always looking around saying, 'Is she here?' It's really bad in the winter when it's still so dark in the morning."

"What would you do if you saw her?" I asked.

"I don't know. My father, he was a farmer and builder in Ecuador and he lived in the country. He told me, 'When you see a ghost, don't be afraid of it, or it will stop you. Just tell it to go away, it doesn't belong here, and you will be all right.'"

"Your father told you that, he said it just like that? 'When you see a ghost...?'"

"Yes," she said with a laugh. "But I don't know if I'd be that brave."

The people at the Netherland Plaza acknowledge their ghost and consider it simply a part of the hotel's history. T.J. Mobilio continues to do research on the ghost and said he would love to see her someday.

"She doesn't do any harm," he said, "and we're proud of her. I'm glad she's here."

Taffy's Main Street Coffee
EATON

SOMETIMES, WHILE I WAS WORKING ON THIS BOOK, I WONDERED IF MAYBE THE SPIRITS WERE HELPING ME OUT; real ghostwriters, as it were. The story of Taffy's Main Street Coffee in Eaton is an example of what I mean.

My wife, Mary, and I had been in Eaton in the spring to investigate Fort St. Clair, a historic site said to be haunted by the ghosts of several Kentucky militiamen killed there by Miami Indians in 1792. After visiting the battlefield site, we drove back through downtown Eaton and spotted the colorful umbrellas shading the tables on the sidewalk outside Taffy's. The shop had an interesting Victorian feel to it, so we stopped in.

It was a Sunday afternoon and we were the only customers. That gave us a chance to look around while we sipped our coffee and nibbled our scones. Hardwood floors, high ceilings, and fan-lights created an old-time, comfortable ambience. We sat at a table by a wall festooned with publicity photos of the many musicians who had played at Taffy's. I chatted with the server and told her why we were in town. She was interested in the project and, as I left, I gave her one of my business cards, *Ghosthunting Ohio* printed prominently across it. We drove back to Athens and forgot all about Taffy's.

Three weeks later a woman identifying herself as Nancy Peters, owner of Taffy's, left a message for me on my answering machine. She had found my card by the cash register when she was cleaning and assumed I wanted to talk to her about the ghost at Taffy's!

Of course, I would have wanted to talk with her had I known there was a ghost there (okay, I can't always find them), so I called her back.

Nancy was excited to have someone to talk to about her story. "I would never have believed such a thing could happen to me," she said.

She told me that she and her husband, Tony, bought the old Victorian building that now serves as both Taffy's and their home about twelve years ago, although they did not open the coffee shop until 1999. The part of the building that is now the coffee shop was formerly a jewelry store. You can still see the place where the jeweler's heavy safe crashed through the floor when Nancy and Tony started their renovations. The owner of the jewelry store had died under "unusual circumstances," and his body was discovered on the floor behind the jewelry counter.

Before they opened Taffy's the old store was part of the Peterses' home, and it was in that section that the hauntings occurred. While both Nancy and Tony experienced the same events, they never experienced them together. Strange things would happen only when one or the other was alone in the house.

One day while Nancy was upstairs, she heard the sounds of her stepson's electric guitar.

"I knew I was alone in the house, so that really scared me, hearing this loud guitar strumming. I went downstairs, but there was no one there. Worse, the guitar wasn't even plugged in. It couldn't have played, but it did," Nancy said. "That was pretty scary, but nothing like the voice that came out from the wall."

Nancy said that a voice she clearly identified as being that of a male came from high up on the wall and called, "Max!" the name of her dog.

"It scared the dog a lot," she said. "There was no one there and yet there was this voice calling him. It was kind of a gravelly voice, definitely a man's voice, maybe an old man."

Tony also heard the voice, but at a different time.

"It was about this time that I thought maybe I should get the house blessed. I have a friend who is a Catholic priest and I thought about asking him to do it."

"Did you go through with it?" I asked.

"No. Instead, I started talking to the ghost for a few days, telling it that it was scaring me and my family and asking it to please move on."

It takes some courage to talk to a ghost and try to make your peace with it, so that you and your resident ghost can "live" together in harmony, but professional ghostbusters will tell you that the idea of living in harmony with a ghost is not a good one. A ghost, they say, needs to move on, whether it is a good ghost or a bad ghost. It simply no longer belongs on earth and needs to find its way to its own realm.

Nancy doesn't feel that the ghost is threatening in any way and, in fact, the activity at Taffy's has quieted down. "But you still feel a sadness in your heart, like something's still hanging around," she said.

Nancy told me that the owner of another old building nearby was also experiencing similar phenomena, and she wondered aloud if perhaps they could be connected—maybe the same ghost visiting both places. I didn't know for sure, but I thought it was possible. Just think of how many places Elvis has been spotted in.

Ghosts are often stirred up when the places they used to know in life are altered or renovated. Such activity seems to make them nervous (assuming ghosts can be nervous) and anxious. Some researchers say that the resulting paranormal activity is the ghost's way of showing its displeasure with the changes in its familiar environment. Maybe this is what was going on at Taffy's.

Even though things are not as frightening at Taffy's as they were before, Nancy said that, "Without a doubt, his spirit is still around. It has been a life-changing experience for me, because it was real."

Who knows if the ghost will make itself known again? Since the Peterses decided not to contact the priest after all, it may only be a matter of time before voices are speaking from the walls again.

United States Air Force Museum
DAYTON

GHOSTS ARE SOMETIMES CALLED "EARTHBOUND SPIRITS," meaning that some psychic ties continue to hold them here in our realm instead of allowing them to pass beyond. It seemed ironic to me that the United States Air Force Museum, whose every exhibit is a celebration of man's ability to break the bonds that hold him to earth, would be haunted.

Yet, it is.

The museum is a sprawling complex consisting of three huge hangars and an outdoor exhibit, all located on Wright-Patterson Air Force Base in Dayton. This was my first visit to the museum and I was especially interested in finding out if

there was a P-38 Lightning on display, the plane used by my
father's photoreconnaissance unit during World War II.

And of course, I was interested in the ghosts as well.

The moment I first entered the museum I felt immediately as
though I had been transported to a different time, a different
place. The lighting was dim with spotlights here and there illuminating a particular display. I was touring the exhibits chronologi-
cally and my first stop was the hall of early flight. The first thing
I saw as I entered the hall was a replica of the airplane built
and flown by Wilbur and Orville Wright at Kitty Hawk, North
Carolina, complete with two lifelike mannequins representing the
famed aviators. When I turned the corner, moving further into the
hall, the lighting faded. Now airplanes of World War I surrounded
me. They were parked on the floor. Spads, Fokkers, DeHavillands,
Sopwith Camels. I looked up and, there in the gloom high overhead, more planes were suspended at crazy angles, engaged in an
eternal dogfight. In the distance hovered a blimp and an observa-
tion balloon. Mannequins clothed in the air force uniforms of
Germany, Great Britain, and the United States flew these planes
or performed maintenance on them in softly lit tableaus.

These old flying machines were incredibly vulnerable. Little
more than canvas or thin metal stretched over plywood frames,
they offered scant protection from the enemy. What would pos-
sess a man to go up in one of these contraptions? What would it
have been like to suddenly hear the roar of a Fokker and the chat-
tering of its deadly machine gun, to see some German ace appear
before you like the Angel of Death he was, and to have your own
gun jam while you sat there in your tissue-paper cockpit, the
flame from the German gun looming large in your eyes?

For all its recognition as the first modern war, World War I was
still as brutal as two cavemen eye-to-eye, toe-to-toe, bashing each
other with rocks. Fighter planes flew very low, compared to today's
craft, and aerial bombardment became a personal attack in which

an aviator could actually see the faces of his victims as he hurled his bombs out of the plane. Dogfights were close-quarter encounters. Machine guns were the main armaments, but it wasn't uncommon for pilots to shoot at each other with handguns.

There was, however, a sense of honor and nobility among the airmen, regardless of nationality. When Theodore Roosevelt's pilot son was shot down, the Germans buried him at the crash site and erected a cross they had constructed from the wreckage of his plane over the grave. That original cross is displayed in a glass case at the museum.

Still, there was no getting away from the fact that this museum was, with few exceptions, a museum to "death from above," to borrow the motto of the 7th Bomber Wing. Although I had always been interested in history and found the museum's displays fascinating, I couldn't shake the sadness and melancholy I felt as I proceeded through the hangars.

I made my way into the World War II section. Here were many of the aircraft that my father would have been familiar with during his service with the 9th Air Force in England, France, Belgium, and Germany. And yes, there was a P-38 Lightning, parked in a row with other fighter planes. The little escort fighter was also used for photoreconnaissance, with cameras placed in the nose, the belly, and mounted on each wing. I took a few photos of the plane to send to my father.

Some people have seen ghosts in the World War II section of the museum, especially at the *Lady Be Good* exhibit, a memorial to the B-24 bomber that went down in the Libyan desert during the war. Six bodies were recovered at the crash site, while another crewmember managed to walk an astounding 179 miles without water through the desert before finally perishing in the blazing sands. There is another story that says an unidentified crewman simply disappeared; rescuers followed his footsteps into the desert until they, too, simply disappeared, as if he had grown wings and flown off. All that is left of *Lady Be Good* is a few large pieces of twisted metal, but some people have seen her crew. Dressed in their World War II-era uniforms, they linger in the dim corner near the exhibit or appear near *Strawberry Bitch,* a completely intact B-24 on display.

It is easy to see and hear ghosts in the museum. Every turn I took placed before me yet another tableau in which disturbingly realistic mannequins piloted aircraft, loaded cargo, repaired damaged parts, tuned engines. Many of the exhibits had audio-tapes playing so that you might suddenly hear a mechanic ask for a wrench, or a pilot chew out a mechanic for a task poorly done. The tapes ran of their own accord—no buttons to push to activate them—so it was a surprise the first time I heard voices talking to me. I could see how someone could easily mistake a talking mannequin for a ghost, especially in the darkness of these cavernous hangars.

Yet, I remained open to the possibility that people had seen ghosts in the museum, and what happened next gave that possibility even more credence. Still in the World War II section, I paused before a German Messerschmidt. The pilot stood outside the plane, one hand on the wing, the other gesturing in a sort of appeal to a mechanic who was working on the Rhinemetall 30MM cannon he had removed from the plane's fuselage. Both men were Nordic blondes, wore dirty mechanic's overalls, and had grease smeared on their faces and hands. It was a realistic display and I felt as though I had wandered behind German lines.

That illusion continued with the next display, which showed a German soldier in helmet and greatcoat pointing his rifle at an American pilot wearing his leather, fleece-lined flight jacket. It was winter. Snow covered the ground. The German soldier had his collar turned up and buttoned so that only his nose and eyes showed. The pilot was making his way to a railroad boxcar that stood on a siding. The door was open and four American airmen, all prisoners of war, stood watching the approaching pilot. One man leaned down and offered him a hand. The lettering on the side of the boxcar was in French and it listed the car's carrying capacity: "Hommes 40, Chevaux 8." Forty men or eight horses.

The boxcar was not a replica, but had actually been used by the Germans in France to haul POWs to concentration camps in Germany. The fliers in this display looked weary and beaten down, but they were not injured or infirm as many of the real prisoners would have been. No doubt, many men had died in that car on their way to the camps.

I remembered that my father had had a flight jacket like the one the pilot wore. Although my father had never been a prisoner of war, just seeing that jacket gave me a visceral connection to the men depicted in that display. I felt heaviness inside me, in the air around me, as though the sorrow and suffering of the men who had actually died in that boxcar had become something solid, something real. In quick succession, I took three photos of the display.

Later, when I downloaded the pictures into my computer, I was amazed at what I saw. The first photo in the group showed a large and distinct orb floating in the air to the right of the open door of the boxcar. It was whitish in color and had spiral bands running through it. With the exception of the orb, the rest of the picture was clear and sharp.

**Some of the many orbs
at the boxcar display in the
U.S. Air Force Museum.**

As I said earlier, many psychic researchers believe that such orbs are actually spirits. Their theory is that spirits are pure energy and that the easiest form for a spirit to take, the form that uses up the least amount of energy, is the sphere. The second photo in the group, taken only seconds after the photo with the orb, was misty and washed out, as though a cloud had suddenly dropped in front of the camera. Yet the last photo, taken right after the second photo, was, like the first, clear and distinct, although the orb was gone.

I didn't know what to make of these photos. The orb in the first photo was not visible to the naked eye when I took the picture, nor was there any evidence of a mist or fog when I took the second picture. I didn't feel any drop in temperature, "cold spots" being traditional indicators of a ghostly presence. At the time that I took the photos I was aware only of a vague feeling of uneasiness, a sense of sadness, as I imagined what these men must have experienced.

As I was on my way out of the World War II area, a squat and stubby rescue helicopter caught my attention. The chopper was painted silver, its name, Hopalong, emblazoned in red letters across its bulbous nose. I didn't know what it was that drew me to that particular aircraft, but I studied it for a while and took pictures. Its shape gave it a comical appearance, but I didn't sense anything funny about it at all. The craft was first used in the Korean War and later saw action in Vietnam. It is said that one of the seats in the cockpit is stained with the blood of a former co-pilot. Could it be that unfortunate aviator who the night janitors see flipping switches in the cockpit, in a futile attempt to get home?

From the World War II section, I made my way into the final hangar, the Modern Flight Hangar. Here are housed the war birds of my own generation, the aircraft of the Vietnam War and beyond. I was already moved by what I had felt in the previous hangar, but now I remembered my eighteenth birthday and watching on television as my number was drawn from a big drum in the nation's first draft lottery. I remembered friends and friends of friends who went to Vietnam and never returned. I remembered the college friend who came back to the United States delusional, paranoid, and dangerous to himself and others. Yes, there was grief and sadness in this hangar to last a lifetime, maybe to last throughout eternity.

Perhaps that is why this section of the museum harbors ghosts.

The *Black Maria* was a ship that gave me the shivers just looking at it. It was a big, boxy helicopter painted a flat, non-reflective black. The big door was slid back so I could look inside, but there wasn't much to see other than electric lines running along the fuselage and a fire extinguisher. But what made this helicopter unique and ominous was the fact that it carried no insignia at all. No pinups painted on the side, no numbers, no national emblems. This was a machine designed for clandestine operations, the kinds of operations the U.S. government would deny knowing anything about if the bird were ever brought down. Think Green Berets, CIA, Special Ops. Those were the men who flew this chopper deep into enemy territory in Vietnam. The patched bullet holes hinted at how dangerous those missions were.

The *Black Maria* wasn't revealing any of its secrets that day. It was enough to know that the covert missions it flew did not always come to a happy end, that men paid the ultimate price for their service within it, and that they may not yet have been discharged from duty.

I made one last stop at the information counter as I was leaving the museum. The museum is staffed by a large corps of volunteers, many of them aging former airmen of my father's generation. When I talked to them about ghosts, most of them did not want to discuss the topic. I could understand why they might feel that telling ghost stories, or even admitting to those

GHOSTHUNTING OHIO   183

stories, in such a place could, in some way, make their own stories of service seem less important, perhaps even trivial. That was not a feeling I wanted to create. So, before I left, I put my request for information about ghosts in the museum in writing and turned it over to the proper people at the museum. From there, it would be mailed to a government office in Washington, D.C., for a reply.

I'm still waiting.

The Vernon Manor Hotel
CINCINNATI

SINCE THE VERNON MANOR HOTEL IS A SISTER HOTEL TO THE HAUNTED Hilton Cincinnati Netherland Plaza, it should come as no surprise that the Vernon Manor also has its own contingent of ghosts. There is no single entity here, like the Netherland Plaza's Lady in Green, but an assortment of various hauntings, any one of which would make your hair stand on end.

Cincinnati has often been called "America's Rome" because, like that ancient city, it is built on seven hills overlooking a river. The Vernon Manor is not situated in the flat riverside area of downtown Cincinnati (the "netherland") like its sister hotel, but sits atop one of the seven hills, affording guests a great view of downtown, the hospital district (nicknamed "Pill Hill"), and the University of Cincinnati. The hotel is the tallest structure on the hill, dwarfing the surrounding homes and professional offices.

The hotel was originally built in 1924 and served as something of a fresh-air retreat for wealthy Cincinnatians escaping the stench of "Porkopolis," the city's huge pork processing industry located along the Ohio River. Although that industry is long gone from Cincinnati, The Vernon Manor still provides a secluded escape from the bustle of the city for visiting dignitaries and celebrities.

The guest list is a microcosm of American history and culture: Presidents Kennedy, Johnson, and Bush (senior), former First Lady Nancy Reagan, former Israeli Prime Minister Shimon Peres, The Beatles, Tiger Woods, Bob Dylan, Willie Nelson, The Monkees, The Indigo Girls, Mikhail Baryshnikov, Jane Fonda, Judy Garland, Pete Rose, Little Richard, Yul Brynner, Anthony Quinn, Emmy Lou Harris, Sheryl Crow, Boy George, The Temptations, Ted Turner, Kevin Bacon, Chloris Leachman, Keanu Reeves, Sara Jessica Parker, The Backstreet Boys, and on and on.

The hotel was also the temporary home for the production of the 1988 Movie of the Year, *Rainman,* and the hotel's address, "400 Oak Street, Cincinnati, Ohio," became a featured line in the film.

With so much history taking place in the hotel, with such colorful characters coming and going, each of them leaving their mark upon the hotel, how could there not be ghosts?

Still, I was surprised when General Manager Matthew Coffey handed me two photocopied pages of ghost stories from the hotel, a nice skull-and-crossbones emblem printed at the top and bottom of the pages.

Matthew had greeted me in the small but elegant lobby and now we were seated in two wing chairs, the papers resting on the coffee table before us. I was skimming them as he spoke.

"I haven't been here all that long," he said, "less than two years, but I've heard many stories. You should talk to some of the old-timers here. They'd have things to tell you, I'm sure."

Matthew was a young man, maybe thirty years old, neat and trim in a blue suit. He was courteous and helpful, as one would imagine a hotel manager should be, but he was also warming up to his role as historian and was frankly excited about the research I was doing there.

"As far as we know, the first ghost report was from the 1940s—maybe a little earlier or a little later, we really don't know. The story says that a bride who was jilted at the altar threw herself out a window on the sixth floor, possibly the window by the elevators," Matthew said.

I was immediately reminded of the woman who had killed herself in the same manner at the Netherland Plaza, and I wondered about the similarities. Maybe that's just the method of choice for suicides at high-rise hotels, I don't know. I know that I could never do that—I'm afraid of heights.

"Her ghost is supposed to be accountable for the things that happen on the sixth floor," Matthew continued. "Doors open and close when no one is there. People feel cold spots in the hall. Lights go on and off by themselves." He sat back in his wing chair and the light overhead flashed in his glasses and was gone. "It's even been reported that security officers have seen a bride running around the hotel, but we're not sure if they're joking about that or not. Would you like me to show you around?"

Matthew filled me in on the history of the hotel as we walked. It was designed to resemble an English manor house and was modeled after The Hatfield House in Hertfordshire, England. The hotel is small as hotels go—with only 177 rooms, sixty of which are suites—but its size, Matthew said, made it more intimate, so the guests felt more like part of a family than outsiders. At one point in its history, many people actually lived in the hotel, and there are still a few who do so today.

We were on the infamous sixth floor. The hall was wide enough to drive a 1967 Caddy through it with motorcycle escorts on either side. I asked Matthew about that and he explained the design as, again, reminiscent of an old English manor house.

We stopped before one of the guest room doors.

"Notice the doors to the rooms," he said, pointing to the curved panel that covered the door, resembling a coffin lid.

"I was wondering about them," I said.

"This is a valet door. See the lock on it? Guests could open the valet door on their side of the door and hang up a dress or suit for cleaning, then close the door. A valet would come around later, unlock the door on the hall side, remove the clothing, then hang it back up when it was cleaned."

"Are they still usable?" I asked.

"No, times have changed. There are always security issues these days, so all these doors are now sealed shut."

A sad commentary, I thought, on modern life. Why would ghosts want to stick around?

"Would you like to see the Beatles suite?" Matthew asked.

How could I resist?

On the door of Room 624 is a big star with "The Beatles" printed across it. Matthew unlocked the door. The Beatles stayed in the two-bedroom suite during their 1966 tour of the United States. Unlike the furnishings in the rest of the rooms, the furniture in The Beatles suite harkened back to the 1960s and '70s. Framed photographs of the Fab Four hung on the walls, and there was a row of books about The Beatles arranged on a shelf in the living room. Beatle dolls frolicked on the furniture. The room brought back memories and maybe conjured up a few ghosts of my own. Mathew locked the door and my trip down memory lane was ended.

We were back in the hall. We paused before another room, where Matthew told me one of the strangest ghost stories I have ever heard. A guest in that room went to bed, leaving his wallet upon the dresser. When he awoke the next morning he found that all the paper money in the wallet had been removed and each one was folded into a "little tent" on the dresser. No money was missing and nothing else in the room had been disturbed. The man reported the incident to the manager at that time. The manager came up to the room and saw for himself the folded money.

"What do you suppose that means?" I asked Matthew. "Why would a ghost do something like that?"

"I have no idea," he said.

"Has that ever happened to anyone else?"

"Not that I know of," he said.

We went back down to the lobby. I had only come up that afternoon from the Netherland Plaza to talk with Matthew—I wouldn't be checking into The Vernon Manor until the following day. I thanked Matthew for his help and walked out of the lobby.

Outside I ran into doorman Ignatius Thornton. He is a presence you cannot forget. Part of the hotel staff for thirteen years, Ignatius knows everyone coming through the hotel's doors and they all know him. He is a big man, solidly built, with a gapped-tooth smile for everyone. We shook hands and I didn't even try to squeeze harder; it would have been a futile effort.

Ignatius must have been one of the old-timers Matthew was talking about, because he had his share of ghost stories to tell me. Not surprisingly, they involved the sixth floor.

He told me that housekeepers had told him about seeing a mysterious woman in a nightgown walking the halls—a woman who would never speak. Could that nightgown actually have been a wedding dress? Or is there another ghostly lady besides the jilted bride making the rounds of the hotel?

Ignatius also had stories of personal experiences that defy explanation. He told me about the family—a father, mother, and little girl—who often stayed at the hotel because of a serious medical condition the girl had that required regular treatment at the nearby Children's Medical Center.

"These folks must have stayed here a hundred times," Ignatius said, scratching the light beard he wore, "and they never had no problems. Then one time they come here and I show them up to their room. I'm showing them how things work—the lights, this and that, the television—and that's when it happens."

Ignatius said that as he was demonstrating the TV remote control, it started surfing through channels without his control. He couldn't get it to stay on one channel. Finally, he turned it off, but the television turned itself back on. He turned it off again; it turned back on again. Then, as the television continued to program itself, something started banging on the wall.

"It was up near the ceiling, a light tapping at first," Ignatius said, "then it got louder and started this rapid banging. 'Oh, no, you don't,' I said. The little girl started screaming. I just couldn't believe this was happening."

He got them out of the room and resettled them in another.

Ignatius said that not too long ago Temple University's girls' basketball team was staying at the hotel. Some of the girls had heard there were ghosts at the hotel and they begged Ignatius to take them up to the sixth floor.

"They were really afraid," he said. "One girl wouldn't let go of my arm. As soon as we got off on the sixth floor, there was this coldness in the hall. We started down the hall and as we got in front of Room 618, there was this loud bang on the door. I mean, *ka-boom!* The girls started screaming and we all got out of there."

We had been standing outside all this time, enjoying an unusually warm and sunny April day. Ignatius had been smiling and joking as we talked, but he became more subdued and secretive as he talked about other paranormal activities he had witnessed. From what he told me, I pieced together that he had been strongly attracted to the occult and the paranormal realm as a youth, that he had become more than attracted by it. Obsessed would be a better way to state it. He told me how, as a youth in Alabama, his family would see ghosts and talk about them as if they were real people.

"I remember sitting on the porch with them in the pouring rain one time, raining so hard you couldn't see a thing, and they would say, 'There goes so-and-so. I wonder where's he going.' A minute or two later, they'd say, 'There goes somebody else,' and I'm looking but there's no one there," Ignatius said.

But Ignatius went beyond what his family experienced. "I was looking," he said. "I had some serious encounters, man. Serious." He shook his head. "It got very physical. They'd just attach themselves to you. You open that door and they will come through that door. I knew what I had to do to get that door shut and I don't want to mess with it no more."

What Ignatius did to close that door to the spirit world was to become a "very religious person for the last twenty-three years." He also served as a pastor for six years.

"No more, I don't want to mess with it," he said.

I didn't see Ignatius when I checked into the Mikhail Baryshnikov suite the next day. On the seventh floor of the hotel, the suite wrapped around two sides of it. I had outstanding views of Cincinnati and the university and it was exceptionally quiet, the only sound the moaning of the wind streaming around the corner of the building.

When I went to bed that night I deliberately left my wallet on the dresser, along with a little pile of change in case a ghost wanted to make a little car with my money instead of a tent. In the morning I found that it had made neither.

A little later I had the opportunity to talk with Charlene Kirby, who had worked at The Vernon Manor for twenty-four years. She was cleaning one of the rooms on the third floor. A short, pleasant woman with Shirley Temple curls, she told me that she had never seen a ghost herself, but that she most certainly believed in their existence.

Charlene did tell me a story she remembered from earlier years. She told me about a woman who lived at the hotel in Room 321 and what happened when the woman died there.

"For a few weeks after she died," Charlene said, "if you went in there to clean, you'd hear the woman's voice, and there was always a chill in the room."

There was another story from the third floor in the papers that Matthew Coffey had given me. In February 2004, a man staying in Room 310 awoke to find a dark figure that looked like a man sitting in a chair that had been pulled out from its usual spot and was turned toward the bed. The ghost was just sitting in the chair, elbows on knees, looking at the man. The man yelled, 'What are you doing here?' thinking it was an intruder. When he yelled, the ghost jumped, then slipped to the floor. The man got out of bed but could find no trace of a person or ghost. The man was scared and sat back down on the bed. As he did so he saw, from the corner of his eye, a dark figure walk by the television, heading back to the chair. The man ran from the room and spent the rest of the night in a co-worker's room. In the morning he returned to his room to find the chair still out of place.

That wasn't the first time a male ghost had been seen in the hotel. A few years back a security officer on the fifth floor saw a transparent man approaching him from the elevator area. The security man froze as the ghost drew nearer. It disappeared right in front of the officer, who then felt a cold breeze sweep through him.

After I had spoken with Charlene I headed back to my room to collect my things and check out. I came to a door with a large window imbedded in its frame. Just as I was about to pull the door open, it suddenly swung out all by itself. I froze. Two little girls, too short to be visible in the window, came through the door.

"Hi, mister," one of them said.

"Boo!" I said.

Woodland Cemetery
DAYTON

IN THE MID-1800S, DAYTON WAS SOMETHING OF A BOOMTOWN and its soaring population soon became too much for the two cemeteries in town to handle. Through the auspices of some of the city's leading families, a cemetery association was formed and rolling, elevated land overlooking the city was purchased for a new cemetery. In 1843, Woodland Cemetery was dedicated.

The cemetery is a microcosm of the history of Dayton. Buried here are figures both important to Dayton and to the country as well. Orville and Wilbur Wright, the poet Paul Laurence Dunbar, National Cash Register founder John Patterson, and humorist

Erma Bombeck are just a few of the influential persons whose remains are interred here.

As you might expect, there are also persons here who are not able to rest easy, persons long gone whose spirits now restlessly roam the cemetery. They were the reason I had come to Woodland.

The main gate is flanked by two Romaesque style stone buildings, one a chapel—with Tiffany stained glass windows—the other a visitors' center and administrative offices. Once you're through the gates the natural beauty of the cemetery surrounds you; the cemetery is also an arboretum containing a wide variety of tree species. The arboretum, along with the tranquil Goose Lake, draws people to the cemetery simply to immerse themselves in nature as they walk the peaceful roads.

I entered the office. The manager on duty was a little man with a clipped, dark moustache and glasses. He wore a dark blue dress shirt with a black tie. A metal nametag pinned to his shirt read Chet*. When I asked him for a cemetery map, he whisked one out of a holder and opened it on the counter before me. Chet was a man who was proud of his work, proud of the cemetery, and very excited to tell others about its history. I spent close to half an hour with him as he pored over the map, marking all the memorials I should visit, regaling me with stories about each of the persons buried there.

I was impressed. The man was a walking encyclopedia of cemetery lore. Who better to ask than him?

"Any ghosts?"

He chuckled. "People ask me that all the time. I've worked here for many years—in fact, I used to give the cemetery tour—and I've never seen a ghost. There was a guy visiting here once, in the mausoleum, who said that he was getting strange vibes in there. He wanted to set up some equipment, I don't know what kind, to see if he could detect ghosts. He never came back, though. It's a shame. I would like to know myself."

"No one has told you any ghost stories about the place?" I asked.

"Not really," Chet said. "Oh, there were some students from UD [University of Dayton] that said they saw a girl walking among the graves in one of the newer sections of the cemetery, and for some reason they were convinced she was a ghost. I don't know if she walked through the fence or what. You never know with the students, especially if alcohol is involved."

I wasn't sure if Chet was talking about the same ghost that a UD student saw at least three times, always sitting on a particular gravestone. She was described as young and blonde, wearing a red top, blue jeans, and athletic shoes, with a blue sweater tied around her waist. The student said that she was crying inconsolably and was oblivious to his presence. The student thought it odd that she was alone and in such grief, and yet no one came to offer help or comfort. On two other occasions he saw her sitting there, wearing the same clothes, crying and unaware of anyone else. When the student brought a skeptical buddy with him to see the girl, she was gone.

I thanked Chet for his help and got back in my car. He had given me a self-guided tour of the cemetery on tape. I popped the cassette into my tape player. But I hadn't driven too far over the narrow roads winding their way up and down and around the hills in the cemetery before I became hopelessly lost. I found myself parked at the edge of the road, looking at a ten-foot-tall granite obelisk while the voice on the tape was calling my attention to the giant marble angel and cross memorial that I *should* have been looking at. I decided to rely on the map Chet had marked out for me rather than the taped directions. I drove with one hand holding the map, the other holding the wheel, cautiously maneuvering among the mausoleums and gravestones, all the while allowing the tape to cheerfully narrate its incorrect directions and inaccurate descriptions. Such confusion. If there was a Disney ride in Afghanistan, I thought, it would be like this little excursion.

Almost by accident, I pulled up right alongside one of the memorials I wanted to see, that of little Johnny Morehouse. Johnny was only five years old in 1860 when he fell into one of the canals that were then common in Dayton and other Ohio towns. His dog jumped in after the struggling boy. It has never been determined whether the dog dived in attempting to rescue the little boy, or whether he simply followed his master in dumb obedience. In any case, the dog's efforts were in vain and, tragically, both drowned.

Johnny's memorial is a statue of a massive dog that drapes one paw over the form of a boy curled up at the feet of the dog, sleeping peacefully. The dog looks out at you as if to warn you against bothering the boy. The inscription on the marker reads: "Slumber sweet." This poignant memorial is, by far, the most popular in the cemetery. Visitors leave toys and assorted trinkets at the grave and the day that I was there, the day before Easter, dog and boy were buried beneath the debris of what looked like a Wal-Mart explosion. A knit scarf was tied around the big dog's neck, as were some ribbons. Strings of brightly colored Mardi Gras-style beads added a festive touch to the somber pooch. Little Johnny wore a knit hat. Arranged on the memorial itself, and piled on the ground around it, were Matchbox cars; assorted action figures; a toy hunting horn, decorated with a Christmas ribbon; gingerbread men cookies; a Barbie doll; a train; various animal dolls, including a lamb wearing a striped shirt and jeans; an Elmo doll; a three-foot-tall devil-red Easter bunny; and other assorted trinkets.

The cemetery manager had told me that it is something of a custom, a morbid one at that, for mothers to bring their children to Johnny's grave as a lesson about what happens to little children who disobey their mothers, although I'm not at all

certain how the boy's accident was a result of disobedience—
but far be it for me to impugn local traditions.

At least one psychic investigator believes Johnny's ghost, and
that of his dog, wander the cemetery looking for mischief. The
story goes that a man who lived near the cemetery saw a little boy
and a dog walking around in the cemetery. He described the boy as
being very young and wearing short pants, something like old-
fashioned knickers. It was not yet dark, but the cemetery's gates
were locked for the day and the man was concerned that perhaps
the boy was lost. He sent his grandson into the cemetery to find the
little boy, without any luck. Then the man called the police. Even
with the assistance of tracking dogs and a helicopter equipped with
infrared equipment capable of detecting body heat, the police
found nothing. No scent. No heat. No sign that a boy existed.

Was that little boy Johnny Morehouse? And if it was, after all
he has been through, can't we just let him play?

Another story, dating from the 1960s, tells of a man who was
visiting the grave of a loved one at the cemetery. As he was turning away from the grave, headed for his car, he heard a woman
crying piteously. Certainly, it was not unusual to hear people
weeping at a cemetery, but the sheer pain and misery evident in
the woman's cries touched the young man and he looked for the
woman. He could not find her. There was no one around, yet
the cries continued.

Baffled, he returned to his car and was immediately aware of
an invisible presence sitting beside him and crying. Somehow,
he was certain that it was the woman. Not knowing what else to
do, he drove home, the ghost weeping beside him all the way.
She followed him out of the car when he arrived home, right
onto the porch where she stood outside the screen door, sob-
bing and crying ceaselessly.

The young man's grandmother heard the crying and told her
grandson that he had brought a ghost home with him. Granny

must have been an old hand at this kind of thing because she went out to the ghost and said or did something—her grandson didn't know what—and the ghost went away, never to return.

Was this the same crying girl the UD student had seen? If so, why wasn't she visible that time? Could there be two crying ghosts in the cemetery?

It is possible that these stories were about two different ghosts. Woodland Cemetery offers more potential ghosts than just those two.

Clement Vallandigham (read more about him in the Golden Lamb chapter) is, no doubt, a candidate for ghosthood. In fact, it is said that he haunts the Golden Lamb Inn in Lebanon, Ohio, the place at which he accidentally shot himself to death. His body was brought from Lebanon to Woodland Cemetery. Vallandigham's ghost has been seen several times at the inn by many people, but it was difficult to find out whether or not it had also been seen at the cemetery. It would be interesting to do a little more research at the gravesite to see what can be discovered.

But if any gravesite harbors ghosts as yet undetected, it would have to be the Stanley family plot. In a little clearing stands the Stanley memorial, an imposing obelisk perhaps twelve feet high surmounted by an angel. Lying flat on the ground at the base of the memorial is a stone slab, longer than a man is tall, engraved at the top with the name of Levi Stanley "of England," who was born in 1818 and died at the age of ninety in 1908. The rest of the stone was engraved with pious passages and homilies, line after line of them. I have never seen so much engraving on a grave in my life.

Stanley was King of the Gypsies, or the Roma, as they call themselves today. In his day, Levi Stanley held absolute power over thousands of gypsies all around the world.

I thought Dayton was an unlikely place to find a dead gypsy king, but further research revealed that in the mid-nineteenth century Dayton was actually a major center for gypsies. Thousands of them made their camps in the city, although I could not discover what it was that attracted them to the area.

Other members of the Stanley royal family are also buried in the plot, including several kings and two queens. When the last queen died, more than 25,000 mourners crowded into the cemetery to attend her funeral while, outside the cemetery gates, even more coaches were being turned away.

I was the only visitor to the Stanley plot that day, but the plot is still considered sacred, hallowed ground to the Roma, one of the few places in the United States to which they have applied that designation. I couldn't help but wonder what magic may have been worked at this spot and may have been working still as I stood there. Careful not to offend the spirits that the Roma believe are still there, I wasted no time in moving on to other, more hospitable sites.

Home.

Southeast

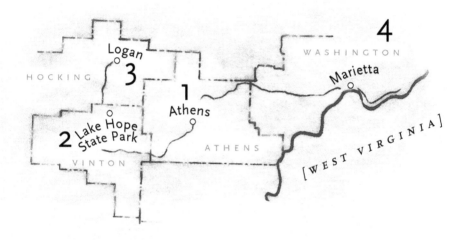

Athens County
ATHENS

The Ridges on the campus
of Ohio University.

THERE ARE SO MANY STORIES ABOUT ATHENS, OHIO,
a place the British Society for Psychical Research recognizes as
one of the most haunted places in the world—and a community
profiled on Fox Family Channel's *World's Scariest Places*—that it
made sense to put them all together under the single "Athens"
heading. Modern psychic researchers believe that the Athens
area contains an extremely active vortex—a portal between our
world and the spirit world that allows spirits to easily travel
between these realms. The Shawnee and ancient Native peoples
before them knew the Athens area as a center of strong energy, a
place in which the spirits dwelt. For centuries Native shamans

and healers sought guidance and inspiration from the spirits here, especially those atop Mount Nebo, the highest peak in the region, at more than a thousand feet high.

Athens's supernatural fame grew in the mid-nineteenth century as the American Spiritualist movement, begun by the Fox sisters—Margaretta, Catherine, and Katie—in Hydesville, New York, swept the nation. One evening, Athens resident John Koons was walking along the road when he fell into a trance and began hearing spirits talking to him. The spirits told him that all eight of his children were gifted mediums, and instructed him to construct a spirit house in which the spirits could manifest themselves. Following the spirits' directives, Koons built a sixteen-by-twelve-foot log room atop Mount Nebo and filled it with assorted musical instruments. One night shortly thereafter neighbors heard beautiful music being played by an orchestra. The ghostly music echoed through the hills and was heard as far as two miles away.

Koons began conducting séances in the spirit house. After putting out the lights, he would start to play hymns on his fiddle. After awhile, horns, drums, and other instruments would join in, played by unseen hands. It seemed to people participating in the séance that not only were the musical instruments being played, but that they were moving about in the darkness as well. A trumpet, or bell, or tambourine would suddenly sound close to a person, only to be heard a few seconds later from across the room or high up near the ceiling.

But the music was only a warm-up for the spirits' show. While the instruments flew around the room above the heads of the participants, pieces of phosphorescent paper would also take flight and float around the room, glowing in the darkness. Sometimes disembodied hands could be seen holding the papers. One story says that a group of scientists studied one of the phosphorescent papers and, as they did so, a hand materialized from it. The scientists examined the hand and agreed that, indeed, it was a hand, albeit a hand without a body. The spirits also wrote messages on chalkboards, or on the foreheads or the backs of the hands of the people at the séance.Through a medium, the spirits claimed to be 165 pre-Adamite entities whose descendent, John King, they said was the first man on earth.

The spirit manifestations at Mount Nebo made news nationwide, and for several years believers flocked to Koons's spirit house to witness the phenomena for themselves.

In 1870 the property was sold to Eli Curtis, a man heavily involved with a Spiritualist group calling itself the Morning Star Colony. Curtis set aside the Mount Nebo property to be used "expressly for spiritual purposes and for a place to form a nucleus around which the City of New Jerusalem was to be builded." A spirit purporting to be "Jesus of Nazareth" visited the founders of the group and appointed William D. Hale and Chauncey Barnes "to carry out the work of our community in and by organizing the Morning Star Colony."

The initial phase of the creation of their City of New Jerusalem began with the construction of a Tabernacle, or King Solomon Temple, an eight-sided structure with a door and window on each side and a cupola on top. The sixty-foot-wide Tabernacle was never completed due to lack of funds. In 1875, the Morning Star Colony disappeared as suddenly as it had appeared, and today no trace of the Tabernacle exists. It has been said that the Tabernacle was struck by lightning and burned to the ground, divine retribution for the colony members' laxity in performing their religious duties.

While the spirits on Mount Nebo may have been of a higher order than typical, run-of-the-mill ghosts, there are plenty of those roaming the environs of Athens as well.

Ray Abraham, a local historian and former fine arts teacher, knows all about them. Ray has lived in Athens all his life and has heard all the stories.

We were sitting in the Athens Community Center. It was a cold and rainy night and there were few people in the building. Ray had a binder containing his research open on the table between us and he was explaining his philosophy about ghosts.

"We all have some psychic abilities," Ray said, pushing his glasses up higher on his nose, "a sixth sense, you might call it. But I don't believe in ghosts. I'm a deeply religious person."

As we talked a little more, Ray told me that he had seen his deceased father and talked with him. It was not clear how he could have had that experience and yet not believe in ghosts. He told me how the Fox network had interviewed him for *The World's Scariest Places,* and how they had taken his facts then distorted and embellished them to create what Ray called "Hollywood's version" of the story. Maybe it's those Hollywood versions that Ray doesn't believe. Of course, working with Fox, perhaps he should have been able to foresee unmitigated exaggeration.

Ray handed me a twenty-page booklet titled *Haunted Athens* that he had put together for a course by the same name that he had taught in the community. I flipped through it and noticed a map of the Athens area that marked interesting sites, including abandoned schools, Indian mounds, and cemeteries.

"What can you tell me about the pentagram cemeteries?" I asked, referring to the five cemeteries that are supposed to form a perfect pentagram around Athens, with its center at Wilson Hall on the Ohio University campus. Pentagrams are symbols that are supposed to draw spirits; only the center is a safe zone that spirits cannot enter.

Rays smiled. "Look at that map," he said. "There are at least two dozen marked cemeteries and there are many more that do not appear on that map. It wouldn't be very hard to find five cemeteries and connect them to form a pentagram."

"But some of them are haunted, right?" I persisted.

"That's what they say. The five that I think make the pentagram are Simms, Cutler, Mayberry, Zion, and Higgins."

I nodded. "I've heard some things about Simms."

"Yes. It's a tiny cemetery, really. Only five people buried there, all members of the Simms family," Ray said. "But there are stories about it."

I had heard these stories. A few intrepid souls who have been able to find the abandoned and overgrown Simms Cemetery off Peach Ridge Road have told of being run off by an old man wearing a hooded robe who appears in a mist. Some say the spectral figure brandishes a sickle. The ghost is said to be that of John Simms, the local hangman. There is a tree in the cemetery that still bears the marks of a rope upon one of its limbs.

Screams are also heard in the cemetery, sounding at one end, answered in a moment from the other side.

One of the most famous haunted sites in Athens is The Ridges, the popular name given to the sprawling institution that was founded as the Athens Lunatic Asylum in 1874 and is now owned by Ohio University. The complex sprawls across a ridge overlooking the Hocking River and is easily identified by the twin brick turrets of the main building rising above the treetops. At its peak in 1953, the asylum sheltered 1,749 patients and was comprised of seventy-eight buildings spread over more than a thousand acres. The hospital was mostly self-sufficient and had its own dairy, greenhouses, gardens, vineyards, and even a piggery.

The story most often told about The Ridges concerns the eerie figure of a woman imprinted upon the floor in one of the old abandoned wards, a woman who died there under tragic and weird circumstances. Yet, the story is not a ghost story at all.

By the 1970s, the institution was known as the Athens Mental Health and Retardation Center and reflected the many advances in mental health care that had come about since the hospital's founding one hundred years before. As a result of these advances, including new pharmaceuticals that allowed many patients to function in society, the huge buildings began to empty out. Many wards stood empty and abandoned.

On December 1, 1978, a fifty-four-year old patient who had the privilege of leaving the grounds as long as she returned in the evening went missing. After an intensive three-day search and a week-long follow-up search, the woman had not turned up. Six weeks later, a maintenance man found the woman's body in a sun-lit room in an abandoned third-floor ward. She was lying naked on the cement floor beneath tall windows, arms crossed and legs composed as if she had deliberately settled herself in that posture. Some accounts say her clothes were found neatly folded in a pile on the windowsill; others say she had dropped her clothes piece by piece out the window to attract attention to her predicament, which was that she had become accidentally locked inside the abandoned ward. The coroner listed the cause of death as heart failure.

The woman's death is strange, but what is even stranger is the impression she left upon the floor. When her body was removed, a stain was left behind that clearly depicts her body. It is believed to have been created by the interaction of her own bodily chemicals with the bright sunlight that streamed through the windows during the weeks that she remained undiscovered. Maintenance workers say that trying to scrub the stain out of the cement only darkens it and that it will fade away in time if they leave it alone.

The stain on the floor of The Ridges, dating back to the building's tenure as the Athens Mental Health and Retardation Center.

There are two cemeteries associated with The Ridges. On a sunny afternoon in October, I walked through the older of the two, located on a steep grassy hillside near the main building. With but a few exceptions, the gravestones bear no names, only numbers. The reason for this anonymity seems to have been to spare family members the indignity and embarrassment of publicly revealing that a family member had been committed to the Lunatic Asylum. It is sad to think that these people, who suffered in life through no fault of their own and endured horrific "treatments" in an attempt to cure them of their maladies, would lie beneath the green grass still spurned by humanity. If ever there were a place where lost souls clamored for recognition, for dignity, for peace, here it was.

The cemetery ends where it dips down into a wooded ravine. A short set of wooden steps went down into the ravine and I followed that path. Here were a few gravestones lying broken and scattered among the trees, some piled upon each other, one or two still standing upright but sinking into the earth, nearly swallowed by leaves and brush. Yes, this was ghost country all right.

There are other ghosts in Athens who do not roam cemeteries. One of them is Nicodemus, the ghost of a runaway slave who was killed by his pursuers at a house in Athens that was a station on the Underground Railroad. Shot in the basement, he died as he was being dragged out of the house. Today, the house on East State Street is owned by the Zeta Tau Alpha sorority and the girls have reported seeing a man over six feet tall, wearing ragged clothing, stalking the halls at night. Others have experienced strange noises—scratching on walls and in closets, whining, and footsteps. Some have been touched in ways that would earn a slap in the face for a flesh-and-blood guy.

A ghost of a different sort haunts the Moonville Tunnel near Lake Hope, only a few minutes' ride out of Athens. In the days when that area of Ohio was producing tons of iron daily, trains used to wind through the little towns of Hope, Ingham, and Moonville often, hauling iron to far-off destinations. Today, the towns are gone, the tracks are gone, and nothing is left but the old ghost of Moonville.

In 1859 a brakeman for the railway had been taking his rest, a lantern in one hand, a bottle of liquor in the other. He fell asleep. In the middle of the night he was awakened by the sound of his train pulling away from the Moonville depot. He rose to his feet unsteadily and stumbled after the train, but never made it. The track tripped him up and the brakeman fell beneath the wheels of the train.

The old brakeman still staggers after his train, his lantern bobbing in the darkness of the Moonville tunnel.

The Castle
MARIETTA

IT WAS AN OVERCAST NOVEMBER DAY when Mary and I visited The Castle, situated on a hill overlooking the Muskingum River in Marietta's historic district. We stood before the ornate wrought-iron fence, looking up at the soaring spires and the crenellated tower. The large windows were dark. Leafless trees flanked the house, their black limbs scratching against the gray sky. A crow sat in one of them, scolding us as we pushed back the gate and started up the brick walk. I had the uneasy feeling that we were walking into an Edward Gorey drawing.

With its octagonal tower, trefoil attic window, and stone-capped spires, the mansion is one of the finest examples of

Gothic Revival architecture in Ohio. When prominent Marietta attorney and abolitionist Melvin C. Clarke built The Castle in 1855, he knew he was constructing a showplace for future generations to admire, but to many of the children who grew up in the neighborhood The Castle was just plain creepy.

Three of those children, now middle-aged sisters, joined Mary and me as we took a guided tour of the mansion. It had been at least thirty years since the women had last been in Marietta.

"We used to think a witch lived here," Arlene* said, referring to Jessie Lindsay, a reclusive woman who lived in the house for eighty-seven years until her death in 1974, just five days shy of her one-hundredth birthday. "Whenever we had to walk past the house, we'd always cross the street and pass it on the far side."

It was difficult to imagine a witch living in the lovingly restored Victorian splendor of The Castle, but the mansion's present condition is recent and is due to the efforts of L. Stewart Bosley and his sister Dr. Bertryn Bosley, who acquired the house after Jessie's death and spent two decades restoring it. At his death in 1991, Stewart Bosley willed The Castle to the City of Marietta as an historical asset and it is now listed on the National Register of Historic Places. Still, Arlene and her sisters remember the mansion as looking a little seedy when they were children.

"Spooky looking," Arlene said.

Even in the absence of cracked windows and dangling cobwebs, there is a strong sense of personality at The Castle, the feeling that the house is keeping alive the memories, perhaps the spirits, of those who have lived there throughout the last 148 years.

Judy Piersall, The Castle's education director and a seven-year volunteer docent at the mansion, agrees.

"You hear stories about this place," Judy said, "but I had always been skeptical of them until recently."

While the mansion's first two floors are open to the public, the tower upon the roof is not. That's what makes Judy's story about being trapped up there so strange. At an October docents' meeting a few years ago, a new docent remarked that she had never been up in the tower. As the meeting concluded and people began leaving for home, Judy agreed to show the new docent the tower.

"There is a door in the second-floor bedroom that opens to the stairs to the attic, and we never lock the door," Judy said. "That bedroom is where one of the former owners, John Newton, died suddenly in 1886. Once in the attic, there is a trapdoor that you push open to get up into the tower.

"Everyone else had already left when I took the docent up into the tower. When we came back down the stairs from the attic we found the door locked. We pushed on it but it wouldn't open. We banged on the door and called for someone to help us, but there was no one else in the house. Finally, we were able to call from the roof to a person passing by and he got someone to come inside the house and let us out. We still don't know how that door locked itself. Maybe it was the spirit of John Newton playing a trick on us."

John Newton may not be the only spirit inhabiting the house.

Jessie Lindsay was a longtime resident of The Castle, and some say she has never left. Jessie was fourteen when her family moved into The Castle, which her mother had inherited upon the sudden death of her father, Edward White Nye, in 1888. In her later years, Jessie lived the life of a recluse and was only occasionally seen outside the house. Her bedroom was on the second floor, but she spent most of her time cloistered in the little library off the first-floor sitting room, a small alcove that could be closed off by two doors. She would peek between the doors at her visitors to decide whether or not she would receive them. Often, she did not.

Despite the Victorian décor and the elaborate red oak millwork accenting the entranceway, the room had a distinctly masculine feel about it. An ingenious collapsible library table sat in the center of the room. A Civil War officer's portable writing desk, formerly owned by Melvin Clarke, who was killed at Antietam, rested upon it. Tall bookcases held a variety of old leather-bound books.

Perhaps Jessie spends all eternity in her bedroom now instead of in the library. Maybe it is her footsteps that visiting Girl Scouts hear walking overhead.

For the last several years The Castle has been sponsoring sleepovers for local Girl Scout troops. The girls learn to cook in the huge fireplace located in the summer kitchen at the rear of the house, learn how to do old-fashioned arts and crafts, and simply have a good time, finally bedding down for the night in their sleeping bags in the summer kitchen and the parlor, just below Jessie's bedroom.

Now a cold light streamed in through the floor-to-ceiling bay window in the parlor. I could see part of the garden outside the window. A large Gothic arch of red oak separated the window from the rest of the parlor. Floral print chairs clustered around a marble-topped occasional table. Against one wall stood an ornate scagliola fireplace mantel, which had been custom-made in Cincinnati and sent up the Ohio River to Marietta by barge. It was a beautiful room, I thought—but then, I had never spent a night in it.

"Every year some of the Scouts who sleep in the parlor will ask who was upstairs walking around in the middle of the night," said Judy Piersall, "and every year we tell them no one. There is never anyone on the second floor at night."

After hearing these same complaints so often, Judy decided to check out the noises for herself. She spent the night with the Girl Scouts on a recent sleepover. At first she stayed with the girls in the parlor, but she was restless and unable to sleep, so she dragged her sleeping bag into the sitting room with its adjoining library. She was alone.

"It was about 3:00 A.M.," Judy said. "I made myself comfortable and was just drifting off to sleep when I heard the sounds.

They were spine-tingling, the eeriest moaning I had ever heard. Human but not human. The moaning seemed to come from everywhere at the same time. It permeated the whole house for several seconds. I wanted to get up and investigate, but I couldn't move. It freaked me out. Then it was gone."

The girls in the next room were all asleep. Only Judy had heard the weird sounds, but there is other evidence of ghostly activity in the sitting room.

A few years ago the staff installed a hygrothermometer, an instrument used by museums and historic sites to monitor and record changes in temperature and humidity in order to help conservationists better preserve artworks and antiques. It was installed in the mansion's sitting room. On a few occasions, the record showed that at about 2:00 A.M.—close to the time when Judy heard the moaning—there was a marked decrease in room temperature and a corresponding increase in humidity. The staff could not find any explanation for these dramatic variances from normal conditions. Psychic researchers say that "cold spots," or sudden temperature drops in a room, indicate the presence of a ghost. Is Jessie Lindsay still visiting her sitting room in the early hours before dawn?

Judy may have been the only one to hear the strange moaning, but several people have seen the lights in Jessie's bedroom. They made their first appearance in October two years ago, during Marietta's Haunted Trolley Tour.

The tour organizers had asked the staff at The Castle if they could make the mansion look scary in the evening as the trolley passed by. The staff placed a dressmaker's form in the window of Jessie's bedroom and shined a floodlight on it. They turned the light on as they locked up the house and left for the evening.

"That night the trolley went by, and the next day we got a call from the tour operator who said the spotlight was much too bright," Judy said. "He asked us if we could turn it down. The next night we used the hall light instead of the spotlight and the tour operator told us it was too dim. No one could see a thing."

Unsure of how to best illuminate the dress form, the staff simply left the house dark when they closed on the third day.

"The next morning the tour operator called and told us that the lighting was perfect! Scary and very effective," Judy said. "And we had not left any lights on at all."

Some ghosts are scarier than others, but how can anyone fear a helpful spirit who can solve lighting problems?

Hope Furnace
LAKE HOPE STATE PARK

IRON MAKING HAS ALWAYS BEEN A DANGEROUS PROFESSION, but in the early nineteenth century it was often lethal. When rich veins of iron ore were discovered in southeast Ohio, iron furnaces sprung up all over the region. Trees were felled to produce charcoal to fuel the furnaces, and the area was quickly denuded. Soon, the barren landscape looked like ancient Egypt, dotted with the stone pyramidal furnaces.

By the mid-nineteenth century, sixty-nine furnaces were in operation in southeast Ohio in what was known as the Hanging Rock iron region. One of the most productive ironworks sites was that of the Hope Furnaces, near McArthur, Ohio. The works were originally named for the nearby town of Hope, which now lies below the waters of Lake Hope. With the furnaces roaring twenty-four hours a day, there was plenty of work for able-bodied men who didn't mind putting their lives on the line. A man could easily die, crushed by a falling tree cut for charcoal production. Worse, he could climb onto one of the charcoal heaps to check the chimney, fall through the layer of dirt and leaves that covered the smoldering wood, and end up slow-roasted. Worse still, a man could be reduced to ash in a matter of minutes if he stumbled into one of the blast furnaces.

Who knows how many men died between 1854 and 1874 in the service of the Hope Furnaces? What is known is that at least one of them has refused to move on.

Towns and railroad lines sprang up to serve the furnaces, which were now producing up to fifteen tons of cast iron a day, making the area one of the greatest iron-producing centers in the world. The furnace was at its peak during the Civil War, providing iron for Union weaponry and equipment. The red glow of the furnace cast a hellish light over the landscape both day and night as men worked around the clock. The heat was intense and equally hellish.

As if the work itself wasn't dangerous enough, there was always the threat of Confederate raiders from nearby Kentucky attacking the ironworks. In 1863, General John Hunt Morgan passed through the area with his Confederate troopers on a raid more than one thousand miles long. The raid began in McMinnville, Tennessee, passed through Kentucky, Indiana, and much of Ohio—from the Indiana border all the way across the state to the West Virginia border, then almost as far north as Youngstown. Already in hot pursuit by Federal troops by the time he passed through the McArthur area, Morgan, who was eventually captured in Ohio, did not have time to attack the furnace, but the threat he posed was real enough to cause the furnace owners to post guards.

It might be the ghost of one such guard who still walks along the top of the furnace, lantern in hand.

His name is lost to history, but we might call him Smokin' Joe for reasons that will become clear. There is something primeval about fire, something that entices us to stare into a fire for minutes at a time, nearly hypnotized by the colors and the flickering flames. Joe was no exception. It seemed that he had a penchant for walking the narrow ledge of the chimney, gazing down into the swirling inferno below, seeing in the dancing flames visions known only to him. No doubt the fierce light shooting up from the chimney rendered his lantern useless.

Night after night, in all weather conditions, Joe would faithfully make his rounds, carrying his lantern and listening for the sound of hoof beats that could mean Confederate horsemen in the darkness.

One particular night the weather was so bad that even Joe hesitated to venture out into the storm. But there were rumors that raiders had been spotted close by. Joe knew he had to go. The rain pelted him, the wind whipped his coat about him, and it was all he could do to keep his lantern lit as he hunkered against the storm. Thunder rolled across the sky, and in the terrible darkness, his lantern was a weak aid indeed.

Joe trudged on through the grounds, struggling against the wind and the driving rain. After checking the outbuildings, he found himself upon the ridge behind one of the furnaces. The ridge was slick with mud and he slipped once, catching himself on an exposed rock. He regained his footing. A crash of thunder split the night.

From where he stood on the ridge he could easily step onto the ledge around the chimney of the furnace. Even in such treacherous weather he could not help himself. He stepped out onto the ledge, raising his lantern high to light his way. Thunder again exploded over his head, this time followed by a searing bolt of lightning that hit so near the furnace that Joe was momentarily blinded by the flash.

One can only wonder what his final thought may have been when his foot, feeling for purchase, encountered only the hot air streaming up from the chimney. He fell into the molten iron below, and in minutes Smokin' Joe literally melted away.

Today, all that remains of the Hope Furnaces, off State Route 278 near Lake Hope, are the ruins of one furnace, nestled against a hillside. Maintained as a state park, the furnace can be visited easily by curious historians—or by ghosthunters. The broad grassy expanse before the furnace may have once contained outbuildings necessary to the furnace's operation, but they are all gone now, as are any other furnaces that may have been in use at the time.

It was hard to imagine the tragic accident that befell Smokin' Joe when I visited Hope Furnace. It was a sunny day, not a trace of a cloud in the sky, and it was quiet and peaceful. Across the street, a couple of hikers were starting off on one of the park's trails, but there was no one else at the furnace.

Steps lead up the hill to the furnace so a visitor can get close, but the furnace is enclosed by a split-rail fence, and an iron grate seals off the furnace's entrance. Inside the furnace was a jumble of stone and debris.

On stormy nights, the silhouette of Joe has been seen walking along the top of the chimney, his lantern glowing. But this day, in the warm sunshine, there was no trace of him. Still, at least one group of paranormal investigators has explored the furnace, crawling inside, and has recorded an unseen eerie voice saying, "I am right here," and, "Cold!"

Odd, isn't it? One would think Smokin' Joe would be plenty warm.

The Inn at Cedar Falls

LOGAN

The Treehouse cabin.

SOME SAY GHOSTS ARE ENTITIES OF INVISIBLE ENERGY that vibrate on a level at which they can be detected by humans. They appear to us in ways similar to music, which is nothing more than invisible energy—sounds waves—vibrating at a level audible to humans. It should be no surprise that ghosts and spirits are often associated with musical sounds—the harps of heavenly angels; the devil's fiddle; the invisible drums, horns, and whistles typically heard during Spiritualist séances. It should also come as no surprise then that, deep in the forests of the Hocking Hills, a guitar-playing ghost would haunt The Inn at Cedar Falls.

Ellen Grinsfelder, who along with her husband, Terry Lingo, owns and operates the inn, said that the ghost was first heard in 1987, the year her mother, Anne Castle, bought the 1840s log cabin that would form the nucleus of the present inn. That original cabin has been incorporated into the dining room of the inn, and its wide wooden floorboards, hand-hewn rafters, and chinked log walls remind diners of a pioneer Ohio long gone, though perhaps not entirely gone.

"It was definitely guitar music that my mother heard at night," Ellen said, "but it wasn't pretty. My mother described it as eerie, scary, and negative."

We were seated at a table in a newer section of the dining room. The sunlight streamed in through the windows, making that area much brighter than the section only a few feet away that comprised the original cabin.

Anne Castle was living in that cabin while it was being renovated and heard the unearthly sounds of the spirit guitar several times each week. The Hocking Hills region is sparsely populated, and in 1987 there were even fewer people living in the area—certainly no one living near Anne's isolated seventy-five-acre parcel of land surrounded by the Hocking Hills State Park. Anne could find no reasonable explanation for the diabolical music. It was a constant accompaniment to the sounds of hammers and saws as the renovation proceeded, and was heard by the workers as well.

"It got so bad," Ellen said, "that my mother brought in a woman who had some experience with entities to cleanse the cabin. They performed a ritual that apparently rid the cabin of the spirit."

The music was not heard for several years, but then, like an "oldie but goody," the music returned in the late 1990s. This time, the music had changed. The first people to hear the new version, a young couple celebrating their wedding anniversary, described the music as warm, loving, and healing guitar music. Nothing scary or eerie about it at all. Was the couple simply infatuated with their own personal love music, or had Guitar Man, as the spirit had been named, truly changed his tune?

"They said they felt silly asking me about the music," Ellen said, "but they knew what they had heard."

The young couple, however, did not hear the music at the original cabin/dining room. They heard it at Treehouse, one of six renovated mid-nineteenth-century cabins snuggled into the hills. These cabins had been discovered in various locations in the area, transported to the site of the inn, and renovated by Ellen's husband, Terry. Now they sport modern kitchens and baths, whirlpool tubs, gas log stoves, and decks. Still, their very walls have absorbed more than one hundred and fifty years of history. Who knows what psychic energies have permeated those walls?

Since the couple first reported the return of Guitar Man, several other guests at the inn have heard the music. So far, Guitar Man has serenaded only the guests staying in the six cabins and has not visited either the nine guest rooms in the main house or the twelve new cottages.

The same gentle, soothing guitar music has been heard around Strongwolf, the cabin that Terry built for Anne after her original cabin was incorporated into the inn. Of the six cabins, Strongwolf is the most isolated, reflecting Anne's wish for some privacy. Could it be that Guitar Man, or to be more accurate, the New and Improved Guitar Man, attached himself to the person of Anne, since she was the one who heard him the most often? Could it be that he continues to play his music just for her, even though she, too, has passed away?

As we talked, Ellen and I ate lunch. She showed me a photo album with pictures documenting the development of the inn, from the original cabin her mother bought to what it is today.

"The inn was my mother's dream," she said, "and she was the inspiration, the spirit behind what we have made it now."

After lunch I asked Ellen if I could walk to Treehouse and look around for myself. She gave me the key and pointed me in the right direction. I went out through the gift shop and headed up the grassy hill behind the inn. It was a beautiful and unusually warm March day, the promise of spring hidden in the buds on the trees and the mossy turf beneath my feet. There is a fenced garden at the top of the hill that produces fresh vegetables in season for the kitchen. I skirted the garden and walked down through a grove of trees until I picked up the path mowed through the surrounding meadows. The only sound was the wind gently riffling through the grass and I thought such music was peaceful enough, even without guitars. The path eventually took me out to a gravel drive that curved down and around the hill. I followed the drive until I came to Treehouse, perched on the slope of a wooded ravine.

There was no one else around as I stood on the front porch fiddling with the key to unlock the door. The only sound was the jackhammer knocking of a woodpecker on the other side of the ravine.

I stepped inside the cabin into a large room that was both a sitting room and kitchen. The cabin may have been originally constructed in the mid-1800s, but Terry Lingo's renovations made it far more comfortable for the modern guest—comfy sofa and chairs, gas fireplace, modern kitchen appliances. It was a bit gloomy without the lights turned on, but I decided to go without them, feeling that somehow they would disturb the ambience of the place.

French doors opened onto a large deck overlooking the woods. I looked out over the rail and could not see any place where a real-life guitar player could hide himself if he were inclined to play a prank upon any Treehouse guests. I went back inside, closed the doors, and then headed down the spiral iron staircase to the bedroom below. There was a queen-size bed and a modern bath with a whirlpool. It was downstairs that I first became aware of the quiet.

That sounds odd, I know, but this quiet was like a well of silence into which I had fallen. I was aware of my ears straining to hear something. What was it? It was as though the air around me was thick with sound that I could not hear. Try as I might, I could not push through to whatever there was to be heard on the other side. I know I'm not explaining very well the sensations I felt in Treehouse, but they are difficult for me to understand myself and almost impossible to convey to you. Perhaps it is because I, too, play the guitar that I was having such feelings. I don't know.

I climbed back upstairs into the sitting room, the cone of silence over me subsiding only a little. It lifted completely once I stepped back outside into the bright sunshine.

I didn't hear Guitar Man that day, but I do think that I was close, that perhaps the next time I am at The Inn at Cedar Falls, I will hear him—maybe even play a duet with him.

The Lafayette Hotel

MARIETTA

THE MARQUIS DE LAFAYETTE VISITED THE CITY OF MARIETTA IN 1825, long before the hotel named for him opened its doors in 1918. But if Lafayette had been a guest at the elegant old hotel, no doubt he would not have wanted to leave. Judging by the stories told by employees and guests of the hotel, his spirit would not lack for ghostly company.

"Although I've never experienced anything unusual at the hotel, there are several employees who say they have," said Cecil Childress, the hotel's general manager.

A friendly, congenial host sporting an auburn-colored beard, Cecil chatted with my wife and me as we ate dinner in the hotel's

Gun Room restaurant.

"Some of our longtime employees have reported seeing or hearing things that they couldn't explain, but I'll let you talk to them yourself," said Cecil.

So I did.

Mary and I were staying on the fourth floor in Room 408, one of seventy-seven Victorian rooms in the hotel. It was a comfortable room featuring antique furniture: a claw-footed writing desk, an overstuffed couch, a side chair with arms fashioned into the shapes of open-mouthed serpents, a large bed with a massive carved headboard. A bank of windows along one wall overlooked Front Street and the Ohio River. Barges and push boats passed by only a few yards away.

Two housekeepers were in the hall outside the room adjacent to ours. I introduced myself, told them about the book, and asked them if they had anything to add. One of the women was reluctant to say anything, other than she had heard stories about ghosts in the hotel, while the other, Ruthie*, proceeded to tell me about the haunted house she had lived in several years before. Then she told me that one of the housekeepers had heard a woman singing and playing a piano, although the only piano is located in the lobby and there was no one playing it at the time.

Both women told me I should talk with Patti*, and they had no sooner mentioned her name when she stepped off the elevator.

"Speaking of the devil," one of the women said—rather carelessly, I thought, given the circumstances. "Tell this guy your story."

Patti was a petite, middle-aged blonde who had worked at the hotel off and on for several years. She told me what happened to her one day as she was cleaning Room 232.

"I was in the room and I had left my sweeper standing by the door. I looked up and saw a woman standing there, her left hand on the sweeper, her right hand on her hip. She just stared at me as if she was criticizing my work, then she disappeared. She looked like Mavis*," she said to the other women.

"Who is Mavis?" I asked.

"She used to be a supervisor in housekeeping," Ruthie said.

"Retired?" I said.

"Deceased," said Ruthie.

Later that morning I met up with Janie Dalrymple, a pleasant woman who wore multiple pins of various designs upon her housekeeper's smock. She was working in a section of the hotel known as the Hoag addition, named for the late S. Durward Hoag, a longtime manager at the hotel. The addition was built upon the site of an old mansion, originally erected in 1835, and is the location of many of the strange events going on in the hotel. The corridors in the Hoag addition seem narrower, darker, and unnaturally quiet. It felt like I was in a chapel, or perhaps a tomb.

"I was working with Alice* that day," said Janie. "I was working the rooms on this side of the building while Alice was around the corner on the other side. I was in a room when suddenly I heard someone yell, 'Help me!' I thought it was Alice and, since she has a heart condition, I dropped everything and ran around to check on her. When I got to the room she was in, I saw that she was calmly making a bed. She had not called out and nothing had happened.

"I went back to work and once again someone called, 'Help me!' although this time it sounded like it was right behind me. There was no one in the room, and again I checked on Alice. Just like before, she had not called. To this day, I can't figure out who was calling, but I know what I heard."

"Did anyone else hear the voice?" I asked.

"No, but I heard it even over the room air conditioner I had turned on while I worked, so it must have been loud."

Janie told me that guests often reveal their weird experiences at the hotel to her.

"They tell me about bathroom doors opening and closing on their own, about feeling cold drafts in their rooms, or being tapped on their shoulders or ankles. The weirdest story was from two women who saw a glowing ball of light in their room, hovering over the bed. It seemed to bounce in the air and they said it looked like a human head."

I admit that after hearing those stories I tried to stay awake as long as possible that night, listening to a church bell tolling the hours, peering into the darkness of my room, watching to see if any of the shadows moved. Nothing happened, although the next day the curtains over one of the windows fell down. None of the ghosts would put the curtain rod back up, so I did it myself.

It's not only the housekeepers at The Lafayette Hotel who are familiar with the paranormal. The restaurant staff has had its share of experiences, as well.

The Gun Room restaurant is decorated in riverboat style. The overall shape of the room is something like the foredeck of an old Ohio River sternwheeler, and the fancy millwork trim and railings would make Mark Twain feel at home. Nautical antiques such as a ship's bell and life ring are displayed in the room, as is an impressive collection of old muzzle-loaders, including a gun that was used in Benedict Arnold's ill-fated 1775 invasion of Quebec during the American Revolution. The restaurant is a cheery and well-lighted place with a friendly wait staff, not the kind of place one would usually think of as haunted.

Waitresses Blossom Broadwater and Ashley Hendershot knew better. Neither of the young women had worked at the hotel for very long, but apparently they'd been there long enough to become believers in the spirits wandering The Lafayette Hotel.

"Mr. Hoag has been seen in here," Ashley said. "One of the girls was working by herself one night. When the restaurant closed she took a break and sat in one of the booths. The place was empty. She looked across the room and saw Mr. Hoag sitting in an opposite booth, smiling at her. Then he was gone.

"Another girl was cleaning up in the empty restaurant when she felt something pass behind her and she heard a voice say, 'Thank you.' She turned but there was no one there."

In addition, Mr. Hoag's reflection has been seen in the mirror located in the small lobby outside the Gun Room.

Blossom and Ashley led me down into the basement beneath the Gun Room. There were some small banquet rooms down there, as well as the employees' locker rooms, but all was dark as we descended the curving staircase. Blossom switched on the lights as we made our way through the corridor.

"One of our hosts met a ghost down here in the locker room," Blossom said. "Sean* was in the locker room alone when he noticed a young man standing there watching him. The boy stared at Sean but didn't say anything. He got up and walked out of the locker room. Sean followed him down this corridor. Halfway down the hall, the young man stopped, turned around, winked at Sean, then walked through the wall and disappeared."

The girls and I stepped into a banquet room. Blossom turned on the lights. Old black-and-white framed photos hung on the walls, many of them portraying scenes of old Marietta and the sternwheelers that used to ply the Ohio River.

"Look at this one," Blossom said.

I stood beside her and examined the photo on the wall. It showed a group of mustachioed men, wearing long overcoats and derby hats, standing with a sleigh on the frozen Ohio River. The sleigh was packed full with boxes and bundles of various sizes. To the right of the sleigh stood two young men.

Blossom pointed to one of them, a youth wearing an overcoat, scarf, and cap.

"Sean said that was the boy he saw in the locker room," she said.

I couldn't see the connection between the boy and the hotel, since the picture was taken five or six years before The Lafayette Hotel was built. In a later conversation with Cecil Childress, however, I found out that another hotel, the Bellevue, had been built on the site of the Lafayette in 1891, but had burned to the ground in 1915. The Lafayette Hotel occupies the site of the older hotel and the mansion built in 1835, so there is no dearth of psychic energy available to its current—and former—resident spirits.

The girls and I went back upstairs to the restaurant. They had one other story to tell me.

"One of the girls had come in early and was alone in the restaurant," said Blossom. "She left a serving cart in the back service hall of the restaurant and went into the kitchen. Then she heard the cart moving in the hall. She heard the wheels squeaking."

"It sounded like the cart was being rolled back and forth," Ashley said, "and through the doorway, she saw shadows moving against the wall."

"She was really afraid because she knew no one else was there; she was alone. When she finally got up the courage to go out into the hall, she found the cart just where she had left it. Nothing looked disturbed," Blossom said.

"Mr. Hoag?" I asked.

"Maybe," Ashley said. "Who knows?"

Housekeeper Janie Dalrymple told me that every year, a woman comes to the hotel with her children and stays in the Hoag addition with the intention of contacting Mr. Hoag. Her children roam the halls calling out, "Mr. Hoag? Where are you?"

Now *that's* eerie.

There may be other spirits at The Lafayette Hotel besides Mr. Hoag, Mavis, the piano-playing chanteuse, and the unknown youth. The girls at the front desk told me that a few years ago someone had taken photos in the main lobby that, when developed, showed smoky, human-like figures that had not been visible with only the naked eye. This phenomenon of invisible objects appearing on developed film or downloaded digitally is said by experts to prove the existence of ghosts. They generally appear as misty, shadowy shapes or, more often, as orbs of light.

The main lobby is a beautifully appointed room. In the grand style of older hotels, comfortable chairs and sofas set amid potted palms and ferns offer guests a pleasant place to relax. Large palladian windows set in the cream-colored walls afford a view of the passing boat traffic on the Ohio River, literally just outside the door. The gleaming pilot wheel from the steamboat "J.D. Ayres," eleven feet in diameter, hangs suspended from the center of the ceiling, surrounded by blazing chandeliers.

I took a picture of the lobby using my digital camera. When I downloaded the image to my computer I was amazed to find two balls of light floating in the lobby. One floats just below the ceiling in the center of the picture, while the other is comfortably seated in a red wing chair below the pilot wheel.

An orb rests in the lobby of the Lafayette Hotel.

I have been able to rule out dust, reflection, or moisture as possible causes for the appearance of the orbs, but I cannot explain what they are or how they got there. All I can say is, if I were a ghost, I could think of no more pleasant place to spend eternity than in the lobby of The Lafayette Hotel.

Levee House Café

MARIETTA

LATE ONE NIGHT IN 1870S MARIETTA, a well-to-do man from the fashionable uptown neighborhood walked the streets of the dangerous and seedy riverfront area. Shadowy figures moved beneath the gaslights—thugs, drunks, sailors from off the stern-wheel riverboats tied up along the shore—but the man was wary of them all, being a frequent visitor to this low-life neighborhood.

At one point, he paused and turned. Was someone following him? He peered through the fog spilling over the street from the Ohio River.

Nothing.

He hurried on to his destination, walking down the riverbank to Ohio Street and La Belle Hotel. The sound of laughter and piano music coming from the building, the yellow light spilling through the windows and glinting off the dark water, welcomed him. He pushed open the door and stepped inside.

Lost in the shadows outside the hotel, a young man watched the older man go inside. The young man wore a long coat, buttoned up tight against the chill rising from the river, and from the way he held his left arm it appeared as if he had something bundled beneath the coat. He stood there hidden in darkness, thinking of his mother, his siblings, and the great dishonor being perpetrated against the family name. He would restore all that, he thought as he slipped back into the shadows, waiting.

"Good evening, Charlie. Take your coat and hat?" said a burly man inside the little parlor of La Belle Hotel.

"Charlie," as he was known to the female occupants of the hotel, and to one young lovely in particular, took off his coat, doffed his hat, and handed them to the man.

Four women wrapped in elegant dressing gowns (and little more) sat flirting with two men in the parlor. Through the doorway of an adjacent room, he could see an older woman, about the same age as his wife, playing a piano. Charlie fished a cigar out from the pocket of his waistcoat. He retrieved a match from his gold-plated matchbox and lit the cigar. He puffed contentedly on it awhile and suddenly there she was, as if materializing out of a dream.

Liz.

Her long chestnut-colored hair was pulled up high on her head, held in place by the silver combs Charlie had given her on a previous visit. The pale blue dress she wore perfectly matched the color of her eyes. She looked like one of the beautiful porcelain dolls in his daughter's collection.

"Charlie," she said, gently taking hold of his hand, and that was all she needed to say.

They went upstairs to the narrow hall with its row of private rooms. Charlie could have found his way there blindfolded, so often had he been a guest there. Liz opened the door to her room. A small oil lamp stood beside the bed, casting a warm glow throughout the room. For the next several hours, Charlie would forget about everything, as easily as he had forgotten his real name.

Outside the hotel the fog thickened. The young man stood shivering in the cold. He didn't know how long he had been standing there, but it must have been several hours at least. He watched as the windows of La Belle Hotel went dark, one by one, and the patrons departed. The man he had followed, his father, did not come out.

So the young man went in.

Slipping through the shadows, his left arm pressed against his chest, he found the door to the hotel unlocked. Inside, all was quiet. He knew where his father would be. He carefully made his way upstairs, trying to step softly on the creaking steps. As he ascended, he unbuttoned his overcoat.

He paused before the last door along the corridor. His heart pounded wildly in his chest as he slowly turned the glass doorknob. Could he do this? The door opened and he inched it forward. The lamp was turned down low, but there was enough light for him to make out the long tresses of his father's paramour and, beside her, his father laying supine in the bed.

The sight of the two of them dissolved any reluctance he might have felt before. With an anguished cry, he pulled the ax out from under his coat and rushed the bed, raising the gleaming weapon overhead. She woke suddenly, springing up in bed, her gown undone, revealing one lovely breast. His father opened his eyes as the ax swung down, a glittering arc in the lamplight, catching him neatly in the throat, the blade sinking down, down, as if it would bury itself in the floor, his head rolling off between the pillows, blood spraying everywhere. And the screaming. Her screaming. The son screaming, until finally the room was filled with people and he was carried to the floor beneath the mass of them.

"And do you know the jury acquitted him?" Harley Noland said to me as he leaned back in his chair. "A crime of passion, they said. Protecting the family name and all that."

I looked around at the other customers having lunch in the Levee House Café, once known as the Golden Eagle Saloon. Daylight streamed in through the many windows, illuminating the old photos and maps hung on the hunter green walls and reflecting off the pressed tin ceiling. It was difficult to imagine this trendy restaurant as a saloon, despite the word whiskey painted in faded letters several feet tall on the exterior of the building. There was a doorway on the opposite side of the room that led into another dining room, an area that had formerly been the parlor of La Belle Hotel. The murder had taken place on the floor above it more than 130 years ago. No one seemed upset by this fact.

"The saloon wasn't added on until 1911," Noland, the owner of Levee House Café, said, "and during Prohibition, it was closed. For a while Studebakers were hand-assembled here. But the other building was built in 1826 as a dry goods store. It's seen a lot of history."

"That would explain the hauntings," I said.

"So would the murder," my wife said.

Mary and I finished our lunch and Noland showed us around the building. A tall, thin man with glasses, with an obvious love for history, Noland seemed more like a professor than a restaurant owner as he gave us a running commentary on the history of the building and its place in Marietta's history.

We went through the door into what used to be La Belle Hotel. The ground floor was now a dining room, the walls painted navy blue with gold-and-silver striped wainscoting. The tin ceiling overhead was an elaborate design of wreaths and torches, flowers and lovebirds, punctuated by suspended gaslight fixtures. A fireplace stood at one end of the room, and I could imagine Charlie warming his hands there on the night he was murdered.

"Shall we go upstairs?" Noland said. We followed him up the narrow stairs to the second floor. "Some of my employees are afraid to come up here by themselves," he said.

The second-floor dining room was small and plain compared to the room below. A single long table was centered in the room and was already set with a tablecloth and place settings. Here, away from the other customers and the staff, the room was quiet. Perhaps too quiet.

"The ladies of the hotel had their rooms up here," Noland said. "Over the years, the interior walls were removed, breaking up the rooms to make one large room."

"Then the murder took place somewhere in this room?" I said.

"Yes, and that's what bothers some of my staff. They say there is very much of a presence here. They talk about having to relight table candles over and over again because they just won't stay lit. Or sometimes, the opposite will happen. The candles will light themselves."

I looked at the candles on the table. Not a flicker.

"Has your staff seen anything?" Mary asked.

"No one has said they have," Noland said. "They just talk about the feeling of someone or something being there. They think it's Charlie."

That idea of an unseen presence is one that many people relate to me as I visit various haunted locations. It is an easy enough feeling to dismiss out of hand unless, of course, you are the one whose skin breaks out in goose bumps or a cold sweat when you go down into the basement, or whose hair seems to stand on end in a dark, deserted corridor. Some of us may be more in tune with the psychic abilities of our bodies and, perhaps, more in touch with the paranormal as well. That could explain what is happening at the Levee House Café.

Maybe Charlie is still patiently waiting for his lovely Liz, lighting candles so she can find him. Maybe Charlie just doesn't understand that he is dead.

Afterword
—by Ed and Lorraine Warren

ED AND LORRAINE WARREN *have been the nation's top psychic researchers for more than thirty years and have lectured extensively at colleges and universities throughout the country. They were two of only a handful of investigators ever allowed inside the infamous "Amityville Horror" house and have the only pictures ever taken inside the house. The Warrens have published nine books about paranormal phenomena, including the best-sell-ing* The Demonologist. *Two movies have been based upon their cases:* The Haunted *and* The Demon Murder Case. *They are the founders of the New England Society for Psychic Research and the curators of the Warren Occult Museum.*

Many people have asked us about whether there is life after death of the physical body. Does the spirit live on? The short answer to this question is yes! In fact, no one ever dies. Of course, the *physical body* will become old, diseased, or withered and die. But the essence of You—the Soul, or the Spirit, or the Consciousness—call it what you will, will never die. Perhaps an analogy will help you understand. You are driving in a car; the car is old and not running very well. Finally, the car (the body) stops running—it dies. You, however, do not die with the car. Instead, you (the Soul, or Spirit) get out of the car and continue on your journey. This is a simplified idea of what happens to you when you die.

One thing we have learned through our many years of psychic research and investigation is that we do in fact survive death of the physical body. It's a sad state of affairs to think that there are people who actually believe there to be only six feet of earth waiting for them when they pass on. That was never God's intention. He has a master plan for each and every one of us. We may not know exactly what it is, but be assured it is not like the end of a movie scene where everything fades to black. We've seen too much evidence to the contrary. We've dealt with literally hundreds and hundreds of spirits. We know ghosts exist. What is a ghost but the spirit of a once living human being?

One should never fear death; it is merely a process of life. It is a necessary step toward our ultimate journey to another plane of existence. You will see your loved ones who have passed on. You will be reunited with friends and, yes, even with pets that have passed on before you. Any animal that had been loved by a human will survive the grave. After all, what would heaven be like without our pets?

We can tell you exactly what will happen to you at the moment of death. You will be lying there, family members all around you. You take that last breath and then, suddenly, you will see a glowing bright light, God's light. The important thing is to go toward the light. Then you will be on the most incredible, most beautiful journey you have ever experienced. Words cannot describe the beauty and the joy you will feel. You are on your way!

Some of you might be thinking, "Wait a minute. If it's so great, then how come there are earthbound spirits? Why do they wander the earth if heaven is so beautiful?" It is because these spirits didn't know to go toward the light. Perhaps they were confused. Perhaps they were scared that they were being tricked. They could have done some pretty horrible things in life, and knowing this, thought the light was a ploy by the devil to get them into hell. But the light is no ploy, no attempt at trickery or deceit. The light is God's light. Go to it. Let it comfort and guide you.

There are also earthbound spirits who believe they have some unfinished business to attend to here on the earthly plane. Perhaps they were murdered, and the murder had gone unsolved. They want to see justice done. Or perhaps they were so attached to their earthly possessions that they didn't want to leave them. We investigated a case in Waterbury, Connecticut, in which the spirit of an old Italian gentleman kept haunting the house. Above the mantel of the fireplace in his house he had inscribed, *Mine, always mine.* He wasn't kidding! He didn't want to leave his earthly possessions behind. There are many reasons why spirits remain earthbound. But now that you know about the light, there is no reason for you to remain earthbound. Still, you remain curious about ghosts.

One of the main reasons for ghosthunting is to have encounters with ghosts. Sometimes, however, the hunter can become the hunted. Graveyards are notorious for harboring ghosts. Are they the spirits of the dead who are buried there? Some spirits will remain in close proximity to their earthly remains, hoping that they can re-enter that physical body and use it in the same way they did in life. Unfortunately, they cannot do this unless they are what we refer to as the "Undead," the "Sorcerer," or the "Black Magician." The man who hunts tigers sometimes finds that the tiger backtracks and begins hunting the hunter. The same is true with spirits. Graveyards are spawning places for evil spirits. Most of these spirits are inhuman, diabolical. They are drawn to areas where human suffering has occurred. These areas are full of vibrations of the tormented people who have lost their loved ones and of the unfortunate human earthbound spirits hovering close to their remains. Evil spirits revel in the deterioration of human bodies, those bodies that God created. They are the dangers that we, the living, must encounter as we explore the evidence of life after death.

We must be extremely careful not to become the hunted. How do we accomplish this? By gaining the knowledge necessary to become an enlightened ghosthunter. The enlightened ghost-hunter envisions himself in a brightly glowing "God's light" of protection before he or she ever enters any haunted area or house. The ghosthunter asks for the protection of God and all that is holy. Remember that these protective measures are only as effective and as powerful as the ghosthunter's belief in them.

New truths, new discoveries, are sometimes revealed only through dangerous encounters. We, as hunters of ghosts, are visible. We are tangible. We are vulnerable. The ghost has the upper hand, for it can see what we cannot. It can hear what we cannot. It can perform feats we cannot. The ghost can come to us any time it wants. It strikes when the time is most opportune for it to do so (usually the psychic hours of the night between 9:00 P.M. and 6 A.M.).

So, if you want to hunt ghosts you must know your opponent. You must respect its powers. The person who makes statements such as, "I'm not afraid of ghosts," had better think twice about encountering one. Knowledge is a weapon, but remember: Fools rush in where wise men fear to tread. Don't be a fool. Be a survivor and an intelligent researcher. Help those who are in the spirit world (earthbound spirits). Help the living reach a better understanding of that supernatural world we will all enter some day.

We have been explorers in this realm for more years than we care to remember. Our work has been exciting, frightening, and even funny at times, but it has never been boring. So, we continue to explore, to research, to delve into the unknown. We are happy in the knowledge that we have found the secret of life. It is that we survive what many believe to be the end, when in reality it is just the beginning.

Ghosthunting Travel Guide

AMERICA'S

HAUNTED ROAD TRIP

Visiting Haunted Places

EACH OF THE HAUNTED LOCATIONS IN THIS BOOK is placed into one of five Ohio geographical regions: Northwest, Northeast, Central, Southwest, and Southeast. In most regions it is possible to explore multiple locations in a few days or a weekend. Some regions may require a week or more if you plan to visit every location. In all cases it is a good idea to call ahead to each of the places you wish to visit to make sure they will be open when you are there.

Happy ghosthunting!

NORTHWEST OHIO

There are several ghosthunting sites situated in the Toldeo metropolitan area that can be explored in a few days or a weekend. This area offers an interesting mix of haunted locations, including an inn, an arts center, and historical sites.

✽ **Collingwood Arts Center** (419) 244-ARTS
2413 Collingwood Boulevard, Toledo, OH 43620-1153
www.collingwoodartscenter.org

The Collingwood Arts Center is easily located off the Bancroft Road exit on I-75 North in Toledo.

Collingwood's director, Tom Brooks, emphasizes that Collingwood is an active arts center where artists live and work, and requests that their privacy be respected. The best way to visit Collingwood is to schedule your visit when the center is presenting any one of its many arts events open to the public. Call the phone number above or check the center's Web site for event information.

✽ **Columbian House** (419) 878-3006
3 North River Road, Waterville, OH 43566

Columbian House is located on the north shore of the Maumee River on US 24 (River Road) in Waterville, southwest of Toledo. The inn sits at the corner of River and Farnsworth roads.

Although the old inn no longer accommodates overnight guests, it is open for dinner throughout the year, except for January. Reservations are recommended. The inn accepts major credit cards.

HOURS: 5:00–9:00 P.M. Wednesday–Saturday

✶ Fort Meigs State Memorial (419) 874-4121
29100 West River Road, Perrysburg, OH 43551

Fort Meigs State Memorial is located across the Maumee River south of Toldeo. To get to the fort, take the Perrysburg/US 20 exit off I-75. Go west on US 20 then west on SR 65 (River Road).

Throughout the year, various events are held at Fort Meigs, including a lantern-lit Garrison Ghostwalk in October. Call the number above to get the most current calendar of events.

HOURS (FORT): April–October, daylight hours; Memorial Day weekend–Labor Day weekend, 9:30 A.M.–5:00 P.M. Wednesday–Saturday, and 12:00–5:00 P.M. Sunday; after Labor Day–November 1, 9:30 A.M.–5:00 P.M. Saturday, 12:00–5:00 P.M. Sunday (MUSEUM): 9:30 A.M.–5:00 P.M. Wednesday–Saturday, 12:00–5:00 P.M. Sunday; after November 1 call for hours

✶ Ludwig Mill (419) 832-8934
canal boat and programs information: (419) 832-6006
Providence Metropark, US 24 at SR578, Grand Rapids, OH 43522
www.metroparkstoledo.com

Ludwig Mill, located in the Providence Metropark, is only a few miles downriver from Waterville on US 24 along the north shore of the Maumee River.

In addition to the mill, the Metropark also has a working canal boat, *The Volunteer*, which offers hourly rides along a section of the old Miami & Erie Canal. A general store sells stone-ground Ludwig Mill products as well as regional arts, crafts, and gift items. Various programs are held at the park throughout the year, including a Civil War encampment in September and the "Ghosts of Providence" Lantern Tour in October.

HOURS (MILL): May–October, 10:00 A.M.–5:00 P.M. Wednesday–Sunday and holidays. (CANAL BOAT): May–October, 10:00 A.M.–4:00 P.M. Wednesday–Friday, 11:00 A.M.–5:00 P.M. Saturday, Sunday, and holidays. Canal boat departs on the hour; charters are available. Adults: $4. Seniors (over 60): $3. Children (12 & under): $2. Children 2 & under: free.

OTHER NOTABLE ACCOMMODATIONS

֍ **The Mill House** (419) 832-6455
24070 Front Street, P.O. Box 102, Grand Rapids, OH 43522
innkeeper@themillhouse.com
www.themillhouse.com

While there are many familiar hotels located along I-75 and the various
state routes in the area, The Mill House Bed and Breakfast in Grand
Rapids offers a historical alternative. Innkeepers Karen and Jim Herzberg
have three beautiful rooms in their converted 1898 steam-powered flour
mill overlooking a side-cut of the Miami & Erie canal.

NORTHEAST OHIO

Before Ohio became a state it was part of the vast territory known as the
Western Reserve. These lands were claimed by several of the thirteen
original states and settled by people from each of them. Most of Northeast
Ohio was claimed by Connecticut, so it is not surprising to find pioneer
cemeteries in this region in which former Nutmeggers are buried.

While the region does have major population centers such as Cleveland, Akron, and Youngstown, there are also numerous small towns,
many of which have a New England feel to them.

You can easily visit haunted sites in the Akron and Medina areas
over a weekend, but you should allow a few more days if you want to
include the more northeasterly sites in a single trip.

֍ **Ashtabula County District Library** (440) 997-9341
335 West 44th Street, Ashtabula, OH 44004
www.acdl.info

HOURS: Monday–Thursday, 9:30 A.M.–8:30 P.M., Friday, 9:30 A.M.–
6:00 P.M., Saturday, 9:30 A.M.–5:00 P.M., Sunday, 1:00–4:00 P.M.

֍ **Warehouse on the Canal** (330) 854-1111
Let's Mango Tea Garden Restaurant, 239 North Canal Street,
Canal Fulton, OH 44614
www.warehouseonthecanal.com

Ken and Margarita Roberts are the owners of the Warehouse on the Canal
and Let's Mango. The Warehouse contains an antique store, art galleries,
and other interesting shops. Let's Mango Tea Garden Restaurant is also

located in the Warehouse and features over sixty teas, fruit juices, wraps, and some of Magarita's native Dominican Republic specialties, including the famous Canawler, a pastry unlike anything you've ever tasted before.

Ghost investigator Sherri Brake-Recco offers a monthly dinner at Let's Mango, along with a lecture and ghost tour in the Warehouse. Call for information or reservations.

❧ Main Street Café (330) 722-2729
17 Public Square, Medina, OH 44256
www.mainstreet-medina.com

This elegant restaurant, directly on Medina's quaint public square, captures the nostalgic ambience of the 1890s. The menu displays excellent and unique entrees such as roasted blackberry chicken, baked stacked tenderloin, and bronzed salmon antipasto. Don't forget the ghost in the basement. Call for reservations.

❧ Medina Steakhouse & Saloon (330) 723-2853 or 1-888-723-2853
538 West Liberty Street, Medina, OH 44256

Enjoy fine dining in a casual atmosphere in this 1858 renovated stagecoach stop and inn. Certified Angus beefsteaks, chops, ribs, chicken, seafood, and pasta are all featured on the menu. The ghosts that haunt the restaurant are not listed on the menu.

HOURS: Monday–Thursday, 11:00 A.M.–10:00 P.M., Friday–Saturday, 11:00 A.M.–11:00 P.M., Sunday, 4:00–8:00 P.M.

❧ Rider's Inn (440) 942-2742
792 Mentor Avenue, Painesville, OH 44077
www.ridersinn.com

Owner Elaine Crane and the spirit of Mistress Suzanne invite you to stay awhile in one of the inn's ten antique furnished guest rooms. Breakfast comes with your stay and there is also a dining room and pub that are open to the public.

HOURS (BED & BREAKFAST): Open daily except Christmas Day. Reservations are preferred. Call (440) 942-2742. Restaurant: Lunch served daily from 11:00 A.M. until dinner. Dinner is served Sunday–Thursday, 5:00–9:00 P.M., Friday and Saturday, 5:00–10:00 P.M. A Sunday brunch is served 10:00 A.M.–3:00 P.M. (PUB): Mr. Joseph's English Pub is open Sunday–Thursday, 11:30 A.M.–midnight; Friday–Saturday, 11:30 A.M.–2:00 A.M.

❧ **The Old Tavern Restaurant** (440) 428-2091 or 1-800-7-TAVERN
SR 84 at County Line Road, P.O. Box 61, Unionville, OH 44088
questions@yeoldtavern.com

Built in 1798 and originally named the Webster House, the restaurant
is the oldest continuously operated tavern in Ohio. The tavern was a
stopover place for settlers traveling west, for soldiers heading to the
front during the War of 1812, and for runaway slaves who rode the
Underground Railroad to freedom.

HOURS: Tuesday–Thursday, 11:00 A.M.–8:00 P.M., Friday–Saturday,
11:00 A.M.–10:00 P.M., Sunday brunch 9:00 A.M.–2:00 P.M., Sunday
dinner 12:00–8:00 P.M. Major credit cards are accepted.

CENTRAL OHIO

Central Ohio is the true Ohio heartland. At its very center is the state
capital, Columbus, with its government buildings and the sprawling
Ohio State University, but this region also contains many small towns
more typical of Ohio's rural and agricultural heritage. Most of the
haunted sites in the area can be visited in three to five days, although
allowing a week would give you a more leisurely trip.

❧ **Camp Chase Confederate Cemetery**
c/o Hilltop Historical Society at (614) 276-0060
2900 Sullivant Avenue, Columbus, OH 43204

The two-acre cemetery is easily recognized by the stone walls surrounding it
and the Ohio historical marker placed beside the sidewalk. There is no parking lot, so visitors must find a place to park along one of the side streets.

❧ **The Granville Inn** (740) 587-3333
314 East Broadway, Granville, OH 43023
www.granvilleinn.com

Granville is located on SR 37 north of I-70, just east of Columbus. In 1924
coal magnate John Sutphin Jones built The Granville Inn, modeling it
after a traditional English country manor. Built of native sandstone, the
inn's twenty-seven rooms and three suites recall a more gracious time
of living. The main dining room is extensively oak-paneled and features
an enormous fireplace and leaded glass windows. The cuisine is excellent and the Sunday brunch omelets are the best in Ohio.

❧ **The Lofts Hotel** (614) 461-2663
55 East Nationwide Boulevard, Columbus, OH 43215
www.55lofts.com

The Lofts Hotel is located just off High Street in downtown Columbus's new Arena District. The boutique hotel features forty-four New York loft-style guest rooms with floor-to-ceiling windows, exposed rafters and beams, and all the amenities of a luxury hotel.

❧ **Majestic Theatre** (740) 772-2041
45 East Second Street, Chillicothe, OH 45601-2543

In addition to being haunted, the Majestic Theatre still offers quality entertainment. Call ahead to find out what's playing. The theater is located in Chillicothe's historic district, where you can find interesting shops and restaurants within walking distance from the theater.

OTHER AREA HAUNTINGS
❧ **The Buxton Inn** (740) 587-0001
313 East Broadway, Granville, OH 43023
www.buxtoninn.com

Built in 1812, the Buxton Inn, directly across the street from The Granville Inn, is also haunted. Perhaps the ghosts travel back and forth between the two.

❧ **Thurber House** (614) 464-1032
77 Jefferson Avenue, Columbus, OH 43215

This is the former home of beloved humorist James Thurber. Visit the home and the literary center, bookstore, and museum. Thurber's story, "The Night the Ghost Got In," was written about a haunting incident in the house, which is still haunted.

❧ **Ohio State Reformatory** (419) 522-2644
100 Reformatory Road, Mansfield, OH
www.mrps.org

This chilling and thoroughly haunted old prison was also the site for the filming of *The Shawshank Redemption*. For a fee, you can join a tour regularly scheduled in the warmer months.

SOUTHWEST OHIO

Southwest Ohio is a heavily populated region of the state, centered around Cincinnati and Dayton. Many of the haunted sites in this region are located within those cities, so you can easily put together a ghosthunting weekend or two that would allow you to visit these sites, as well as some of the other attractions the region has to offer.

❧ **Amber Rose European Restaurant** (937) 228-2511
1400 Valley Street, Dayton, OH 45404

Amber Rose (along with its resident ghost) serves the best Eastern European food in Ohio.
    HOURS: Monday, 11:00 A.M.–2:00 P.M.; Tuesday–Thursday, 11 A.M.–9 P.M.; Friday and Saturday, 11 A.M.–10 P.M. Closed Sunday.

❧ **Cincinnati Art Museum** (513) 721-ARTS
953 Eden Park Drive, Eden Park, Cincinnati, OH 45202
www.cincinnatiartmuseum.com

The Cincinnati Art Museum is located in Eden Park, easily accessible from I-71. Be sure to stop by the park's Krohn Conservatory as well.
    HOURS: Tuesday and Thursday–Sunday, 11:00 A.M.–5:00 P.M., Wednesday, 11:00 A.M.–9:00 P.M. Closed Monday.

❧ **Cincinnati Music Hall** (513) 744-3344
1243 Elm Street, Cincinnati, OH 45210
www.cincinnatiarts.org/venues/musichall

Cincinnati Music Hall is in downtown Cincinnati and can be reached from either I-71 or I-75. This is home to both the Cincinnati Symphony Orchestra and the Cincinnati Ballet.

❧ **Golden Lamb Inn** (513) 932-5065
27 South Broadway, Lebanon, OH 45036
www.goldenlamb.com

The two-story Federal-style inn was built in 1815, replacing Jonas Seaman's original 1803 log tavern. The inn, which still rents rooms, also houses a Shaker museum and a fine collection of Currier and Ives prints.

❧ **Heritage Village Museum** (513) 563-4464
Sharon Woods Park, Sharonville, OH
www.heritagevillagecincinnati.org/heritagevillage.htm

Eleven historic nineteenth-century buildings from throughout Ohio have been brought to Sharon Woods Park and renovated. Guides and special events at the village re-create days gone by for modern visitors. Sharon Woods Park is approximately one mile south of I-275 (Exit 46) on SR 42.

HOURS: May–October: Wednesday–Saturday, 12:00–4:00 P.M., Sunday, 1:00–5:00 P.M.; April, November, December: Saturday 12:00–4:00 P.M., Sunday, 1:00–5:00 P.M. Admission Adults: $7. Seniors: $6. Children (ages 5– 12): $5. Children 4 & under: free.

❧ Taffy's Main Street Coffee (937) 456-9300
123 East Main Street, Eaton, OH 45320
www.taffyscoffee.com

Taffy's is located in Eaton's historic downtown on East Main Street (SR 35), twenty minutes east of Dayton, and is also easily accessible from I-70. Come for the coffee, chess, open mic, live entertainment, and, of course, the ghost.

HOURS: Monday–Wednesday, 6:00 A.M.–8:00 P.M., Thursday–Friday, 6:00 A.M.–11:00 P.M., Saturday, 8:00 A.M.–midnight.

❧ U.S. Air Force Museum (937) 255-3286
1100 Spaatz Street, Wright-Patterson Air Force Base, Dayton, OH 45433
www.wpafb.af.mil/museum

More than three hundred aircraft and missiles are on display at the museum and, if you look closely, you may spot one of the ghostly aviators who still await their orders. The base and museum are easily accessed from I-75.

HOURS: 9:00 A.M.–5:00 P.M. Daily admission: free.

❧ Ye Olde Trail Tavern (937) 767-7448
228 Xenia Avenue, Yellow Springs, OH 45387

Located in King's Yard
HOURS: Monday–Saturday, 11:30 A.M.–11:00 P.M., Sunday, 12:30–6:30 P.M.

SOUTHEAST OHIO

The modern state of Ohio began here along the Ohio River when eighteenth-century settlers laid out the city of Marietta. Such a long history provides plenty of ghosts. Most of the haunted locations in this region are found in Marietta and nearby Athens. They can easily be explored in a few days or a weekend, especially the Marietta sites, which are located within blocks of each other.

Southeast Ohio is also known as Ohio's "Nature Corner." The region boasts many state parks, including the beautiful Hocking Hills State Park, and both state and national forests, enough for any nature lover or outdoor enthusiast.

❧ The Castle (740) 373-4180
418 Front Street, Marietta, OH 45750
www.mariettacastle.org

The main thoroughfare through downtown Marietta is SR 7, which is easily accessed from I-77 to the east or SR 50 to the west. Front Street runs parallel to, and only a few blocks south of, SR 7.

The Castle recently added a "Traditions of Halloween" event that emphasizes some of the strange occurrences at the old mansion. Call the number above for more information.

HOURS: April–May and September–December, Monday, Thursday, Friday, 10:00 A.M.–4:00 P.M., Saturday–Sunday, 1:00–4:00 P.M.; June–August, Monday–Friday, 10:00 A.M.–4:00 P.M., Saturday–Sunday, 1:00–4:00 P.M.; January–March: The Castle is open for group tours, school tours and programs, and scheduled events. Admission is charged.

❧ The Inn at Cedar Falls (740) 385-7489 or 1-800-65-FALLS
21190 SR 374, Logan, OH 43138
www.innatcedarfalls.com

Ellen Grinsfelder and Terry Lingo are your hosts at The Inn at Cedar Falls, located only a stone's throw from the scenic attractions of Hocking Hills State Park. Within a three-mile radius of the inn can be found Ash Cave, Old Man's Cave, and, of course, Cedar Falls. The inn is located on SR 374 about an hour-and-a-half drive from Columbus, two and a half hours from Cincinnati, and four hours from Cleveland. Guests can make reservations for the six reconstructed 1840s cabins, nine guest rooms, or twelve new cottages. Daytrippers can stop by for lunch or dinner (reservations requested).

❧ **Lake Hope Furnace** (740) 596-5253
Lake Hope State Park, 27331 SR 278, McArthur, OH 45651

The tiny town of Hope now lies beneath the waters of Lake Hope in the state park by the same name. All that remains is a rundown cemetery and the ruins of the Hope Furnace. The furnace is located in the park and is open during daylight hours throughout the year. There is a parking lot across the street from the furnace. There are some hiking trails that can be accessed from the lot as well. The park itself is 26,824 acres of woods and lake in Zaleski State Forest, and has both cabins and tent sites available for rent.

❧ **The Lafayette Hotel** (740) 373-5522
101 Front Street, Marietta, OH 45750
www.lafayettehotel.com

The Lafayette Hotel is located at the end of Front Street, on the bank of the Ohio River.

With its comfortable rooms, lounge, and full-service restaurant, the hotel makes an excellent base for your Marietta ghosthunting activities. There is free off-street parking and you are close to the many shops and restaurants along Front Street.

❧ **Levee House Café** (740) 374-CAFE
127 Ohio Street, Marietta, OH 45750

Levee House Café is located across the street from The Lafayette Hotel. Ohio Street dead-ends at the bank of the Ohio River. The building faces the river and its brick façade is visible from the hotel lobby.

Ghostly Resources

ONLINE RESOURCES

All About Ghosts
www.allaboutghosts.com

This site covers ghostly events throughout the United States and features ghost stories, photos, and a state-by-state index of haunted locations.

Ghastly Ohio
www.geocities.com/muzikmann1000

The site contains information on haunted Ohio locations.

Ghosts of Ohio
www.ghostsofohio.org

This group will investigate haunted places. The Web site has news and information about Ohio haunts.

Haunted Marietta
www.hauntedmarietta.com

With information about haunted places in Marietta, this site also offers a video for sale about these places.

International Ghosthunters Society
www.ghostweb.com

The ICHS was founded by Drs. Dave Oester and Sharon Gill. Their Web site has over 9,000 photos, a newsletter, and also offers a home-study course to become a Certified Ghosthunter.

Majda
www.majda.net

Based in Alliance, Ohio, Majda investigates hauntings throughout the U.S. The site contains a gallery of photos, ghost stories, and news about public ghost hunts.

The Ohio Ghosthunters Society
www.ohioghs.com

This extensive site has many stories and photos, a glossary of paranormal terms, and ghosthunting tips.

Ohio Ghost Researchers
www.ohio-ghost-researchers.com

This group will investigate haunted places. The site has news, stories, and "Ghosthunting 101."

Ohio Paranormal Investigation Network (O.P.I.N.)
www.angelfire.com/oh3/opin/

Although this group is no longer conducting paranormal investigations, the site takes a scientific approach to ghosthunting and provides useful information for the novice ghosthunter.

The Shadowlands Ghosts & Hauntings
http://theshadowlands.net/ghost/

More than 7,400 true ghost stories are collected on this site, which covers all of the United States.

Spiritseekers of Ohio
www.spiritseekersofohio.net

This inclusive site offers articles, forums, books, and information about haunted locations. Spiritseekers will also conduct paranormal investigations. Three partner ghost groups are linked to the Web site under "Partner Groups." They are:
- Ghosteology—paranormal events in the Akron and Cuyahoga Valley.
- Spirits in the Sky—Mt. Vernon area ghosts and hauntings.
- North Coast Ghosthunters—investigating the Cleveland and north coast areas of the state.

GHOSTLY PEOPLE

Sherri Brake-Recco (330) 854-0956
riverstx@sssnet.com

Sherri is a registered ghost investigator and also conducts a ghost talk and ghosthunt, along with dinner, at the Warehouse on the Canal in Canal Fulton.

Psychic Sonya (330) 667-0009
psychicsonya@msn.com
www.HauntedClevelandTours.com

Sonya is a psychic and ghostbuster. She is also a Tarot card reader and a practitioner of Native American hand trembling, an ancient art used to read a person's energy or aura. See her Web site for information on haunted tours.

www.ingramcontent.com/pod-product-compliance
Lightning Source LLC
Jackson TN
JSHW011933131224
75386JS00041B/1364